Leominster Revisited

Leominster Revisited

by

Tim Ward

Logaston Press

LOGASTON PRESS
Little Logaston, Woonton, Almeley,
Herefordshire HR3 6QH
www.logastonpress.co.uk

First published by Logaston Press 2009

ISBN 1 978 1 906663 28 5

Set in Minion Pro by Logaston Press
and printed in Great Britain by
Bell & Bain Ltd., Glasgow

Contents

Acknowledgements

After 35 years collecting Herefordshire postcards, photographs and ephemera, I decided to sell an album containing the Leominster material so that I could concentrate during my retirement years on researching social history in the Ross area. I approached an old Leominster acquaintance with the album. Imagine my surprise when he responded 'You don't want to sell that, Tim. Why not write a book on Leominster instead?' *Leominster Revisited* is the result.

It seems somewhat superfluous to write an introduction to a book where I hope the images speak for themselves. I am, however, especially grateful to all the photographers – some known, some sadly forgotten – without whose work this book would have been impossible. My gratitude extends to all my friends who have freely and generously allowed my use of their detailed knowledge; not forgetting Roger Barrett for his technical assistance and my editor Ron Shoesmith. I must also include all the staff in Leominster Library, Leominster Folk Museum, Hereford Reference Library and Hereford Records Office (HRO), who were always cheerfully ready to try to answer my strange requests or point me towards the source of the information I sought. Thanks also to all the Leominster men and women I stopped in their streets, shops, offices, and churches to ask directions or for information. Such chance encounters often developed into informative chats once I had explained myself. My sincere thanks to you all, for my knowledge of your town was incredibly scanty. With your help I hope I have done justice to the photographic echoes of Leominster's townsfolk and their history and the help the present generations of Leominster people have given me. My apologies for any mistakes which are mine alone. Thanks, of course, to my wife, Shirley, for her never-failing support and encouragement.

My acknowledgements extend especially to John Eisel and Stuart Webb, whose knowledge of Herefordshire's early photographers is far greater than mine. I have tried to contact everyone who may have copyright on the photographs used, and apologise for any infringements I may have inadvertently committed. Inevitably my researches have overlapped other authors' work – where we have drawn different conclusions, I hope we can agree to differ.

The following have been consulted in the course of my research:

The Leominster News, Hereford Times, Hereford Journal newspapers
Slater's, Pigot's, Jakeman and Carver's, and Kelly's *Directories*
French Barns, Cambridge Rolls and Register Grates by Ann Malpas
The Town in the Marches by Norman C. Reeves
The Leominster Guide by the Revd J. Williams (Leominster Folk Museum)
Leominster by Eric Turton
Mrs Barling née *De'Ath*, George Court
Leominster Golf Club, Celebrating Forty Years
Ron Shoesmith and Roger Broomfield collections
Mary and Richard Wheeler
Leominster Secondary School Governors Minute Books in HRO.

Introduction – This is Leominster

Of the seven towns in the county of Herefordshire, Leominster is second in size only to the City of Hereford. Built on the ancient road that followed the Welsh border, it has existed as a market town for at least two thousand years, serving the varied needs of the people of the surrounding rich farmlands of the Lugg valley. These farms still produce corn, fruit, cider, cattle and sheep in abundance, though the emphasis and methods have changed with the years. This agricultural wealth was, and still is, the basis of its merchants' prosperity and the magnificence of Leominster's Priory Church, dedicated to Saints Peter and Paul, derived from the same source. The picturesque mixture of timbered and Georgian buildings around the town centre still exudes a feeling of the vigorous prosperity of the years when they were built. Free car parking and this pleasant ambience attracts local people and tourists alike to sample what the town has to offer. Close to the town centre the recreation grounds at the Grange (named from the tithe barn which once stood there), where cricket and archery matches were once held, now offer a pleasant park for quiet escape from the bustle of the town. Here too the splendid old oak market house, dated 1633, was re-erected after its rescue from oblivion and removal from the town centre in 1863. Renamed Grange Court, first as a private house and later as offices, it has continued to enhance its surroundings.

Change being a natural part of life, in business as well as in day to day living, Leominster's shops and businesses have altered with the years to cater for a changing market. Specialist and antique shops abound. Only a fortunate few family firms have survived more or less intact from the period that most of these photographs and advertisements portray. A hundred years into the future our great-grandchildren will regard photographs of the present town with the same nostalgia as that with which we view these glimpses of a nearly forgotten age. Communication with the rest of the country had been slow and expensive, as not even the proposed canal connection to the River Severn and the national canal network leading from it had been achieved. After the arrival of the railway in 1853, however, new markets for local farm produce were readily available in the manufacturing towns of the Midlands and north of England. In return manufactured goods flowed in cheaply. Businesses grew and the town's varied clubs flourished. Independently minded congregations built their own denominational churches to be free of the Church of England's theocratic embrace. However, Leominster had become more dependent on nationwide economic pressures and the 1861 population of 5,658 had only risen to 5,707 by 1941, due mainly to emigration. In the present prosperous period the population has doubled since then.

This book is dedicated to the memory of those photographers of the nineteenth and twentieth centuries who left a superb heritage of photographs that have made this and similar books possible.
Without their efforts we would all be much the poorer.

Postcard Publishers and Early Photographers

Some of the postcard publishers in Leominster between 1900 and 1940 were also photographers. The dates shown are when they were known to have published postcards.

Frank A. Blacklock, bookseller and stationer, Mortimer Press, South Street. 1902-04.
Alfred De'Ath, photographer, 22 Burgess Street. 1905-11, then at 7 Broad Street until his death in 1930. Continued by his widow Margaret, 1930-1940.
Frederick Arthur Dalley, printer, newsagent and stationer, with premises at 12 Drapers Lane, 13 High Street and 10 South Street. 1902-41.
Denbee Studios, 14 Broad Street.
John Harrison, tobacconist, 2 South Street. 1907-37.
John Heffernan, photographer, Claremont, Bargates. 1902-10.
Leominster News, 27 Drapers Lane. 1904-05.
Henry T. Winterbourne, photographer, 36 Broad Street. 1890-1926. It is possible that Amy, his daughter, continued his photographic business from 1911 to 1926 after his retirement in 1904.
Orphans Printing Press, 10 and 12 Broad Street. 1904-37.
A.E. Phillips. 1905.

A number of local businesses published advertising cards to promote their goods and services:

Albert J. Hewitt, china and hardware shop, 3-7 Drapers Lane.
Reg Preece, stationer, 6 Corn Street.
Newman and Co., grocer, 14 Broad Street.
John Smith and Son, draper, Victoria House, Corn Square.
William George Storr-Barber, 147 Bargates and Etnam Street, monumentalist.
George Felton Hinton, animal feed merchant and baker, Rainbow Street and 8 West Street.
The Talbot Hotel.

Early Photographers

Edward Juson Evans, 36 South Street, 1867; 22 Burgess Street, 1870s-1905. His business was eventually taken over by De'Ath.
Robert Jones, 36 Broad Street. 1863-1890.
Thomas Henry Winterbourne, 1890-1910, when his daughter, Amy, took the business over on his retirement.

Streets and Traders

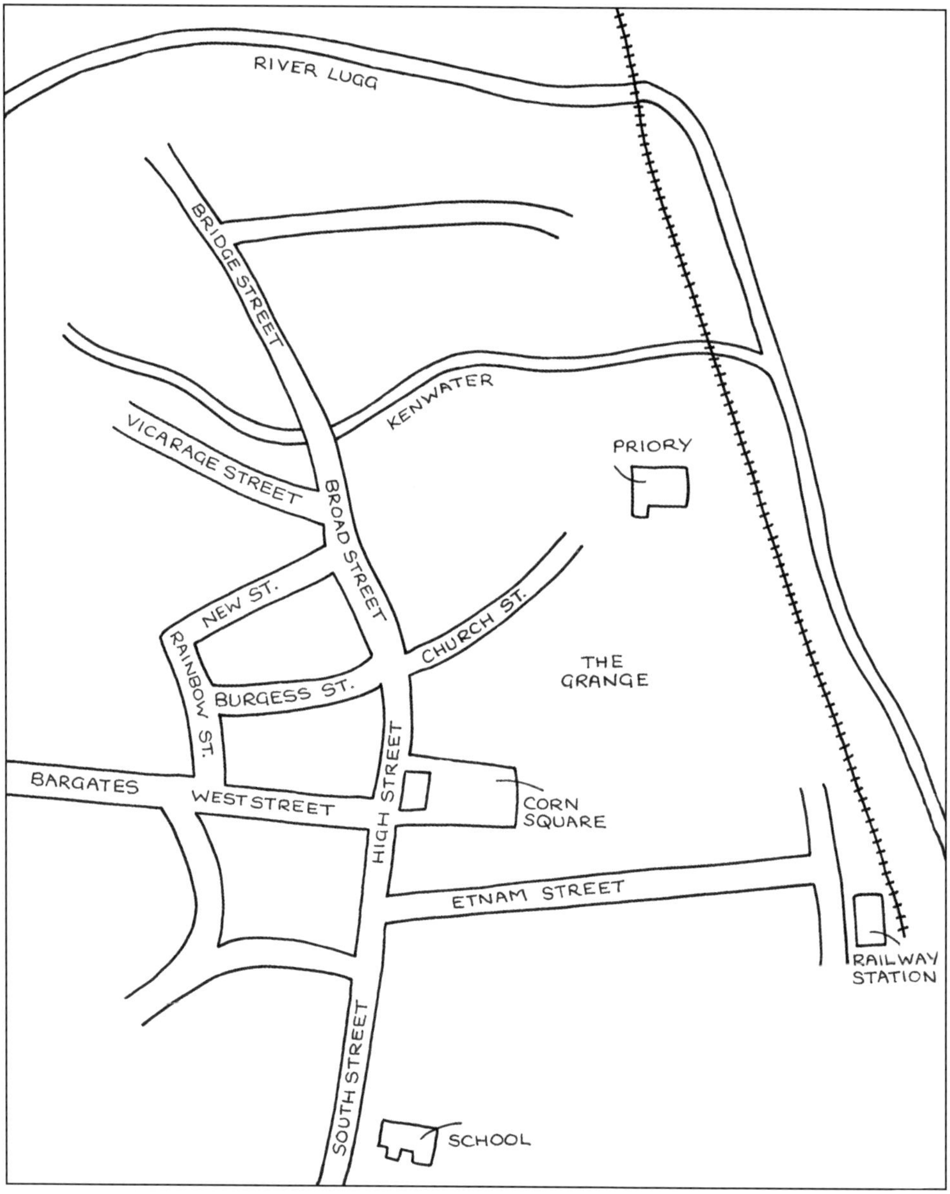

Plan showing Leominster's main streets

Bridge Street, Vicarage Street, Floods and Water

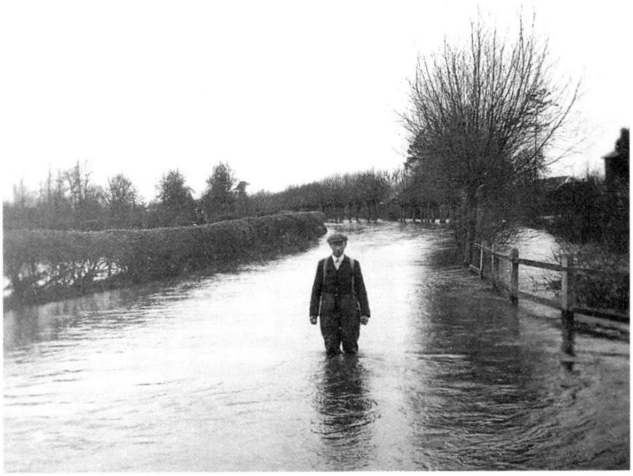

During the 1910 floods an intrepid pedestrian ignores the danger and wades knee-deep along the Eyton road through the flood water for the benefit of an unknown photographer.

Leominster's name seems to have developed from the Saxon word 'minster' (a mother church) and the Celtic word 'leon' (meaning 'among the streams or waters' or 'in the marshes'). Taken with the parish's size – seven miles long by four wide – and the church's proximity to the original braided course of the River Lugg and the Pinsley Brook, and with the River Arrow and the Ridgemoor Brook not far away, all meandering through what was originally a wide marshy valley, this appears a likely derivation.

In the northern part of the town the River Lugg flowed close to the Eyton road with the inevitable risk of serious flooding in the area after periods of heavy rainfall. The constant flooding blighted the lives of the inhabitants of the low-lying areas in Mill Street, Bridge Street, and the Marsh. The inhabitants became accustomed to moving furniture upstairs to safety and the unpleasant task of drying up after the repeated floods, which occurred sometimes six or seven times a year. Following a long, cold winter, the floods in 1947 were particularly deep, long-lasting and unpleasant.

In 1961, Leominster's Mayor, Sidney Robert Booth, inaugurated a flood relief scheme, which received government approval in 1963. Frank Dale, Chairman of the River Lugg Internal Drainage Board, collaborated with Bob Booth, a civil engineer, and Frank Hodges, Chief Engineer of the Wye Drainage Authority, on the detailed plans. Much of the work was carried out by the town's own local labour over the next six years. A short, new channel diverted the Pinsley Brook away from its previous course along the side of Vicarage Street into the Kenwater. The major part of the scheme involved cutting a new course for the River Lugg to the north of the town beyond the old railway embankment, which was incorporated into the scheme as a levee to keep flood water away from built-up areas. The work involved cutting deeper channels, an extra bridge, spillways and a split weir to permanently protect houses from the mud, filth and misery caused by the never-ending flooding. The people living in the houses on the flood-plain regarded the £500,000 as money well spent. For their lasting contribution to the general health and safety of the people of Leominster by eliminating these devastating floods, Booth, Dale and Hodges deserve better recognition than the vandalized plaque now kept in the Council Offices in West Street.

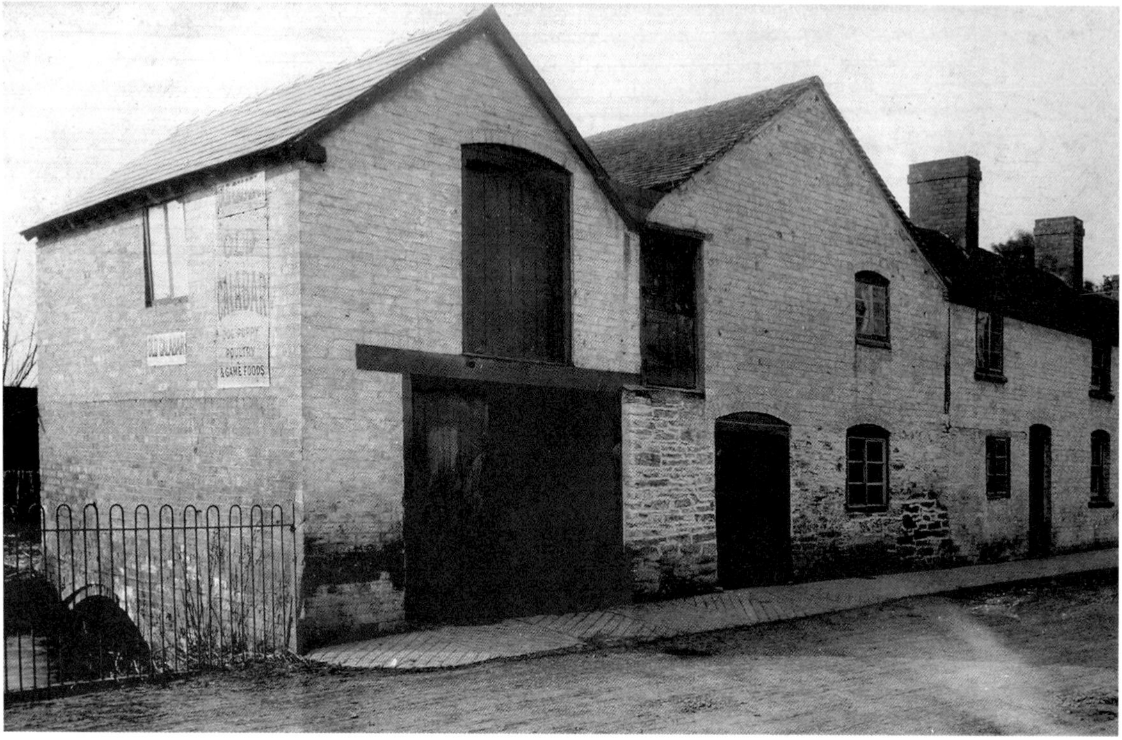

At the time of writing, Frederick Gillum's old steam and water mill at No.99a Bridge Street (now Old Ludlow Road) is being demolished. The mill was built over a leat from the River Lugg, harnessing the power of the stream to drive the water-wheel whose outfall is just visible on the left of the mill building. The advertisement on the side of the building reads 'Old Calabar. Dog, Puppy, Poultry, and Game Foods'. New housing has replaced the row of cottages on the right of this photograph, which was taken in 1909.

The *Leominster News* reported that the floods in December 1910 were the worst since 1852 and took a fortnight to subside. Flood water was 2½ to 3 feet deep in parts of Bridge Street with about one hundred cottages affected. Sympathetic local businessmen started a Flood Relief Fund for a soup kitchen to provide hot food for the sufferers, and when the flood water subsided each affected householder was given two hundred weight of coal to help dry out their property. Teams of rescuers with ladders and horse-drawn carts helped marooned people from their cottages.

Local stories suggest that people became so used to the floods that they simply opened their front and back doors to let the river water run through their houses!

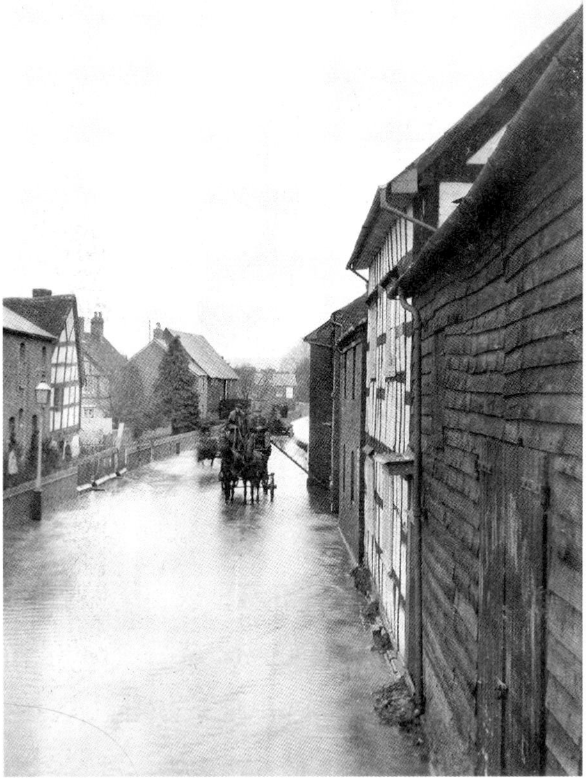

Left: *A flooded part of Bridge Street looking south towards the town where the houses have now been demolished. A leat from the Lugg ran beside the road providing power for two water mills. Unfortunately, after heavy rain in the Lugg's extensive catchment area, which stretched from central Wales, it also helped carry flood water to this densely populated low-lying part of the town.*

Below: *A more pleasant picture looking north along Bridge Street in the early 20th century. The roof of the half-timbered house now seems to show more of a lean, and the cottages to its left have been demolished to make an access road to the new houses in Ridgemoor Road.*

On the opposite side of the road iron railings fenced off the River Lugg, across which a number of small bridges led to riverside houses.

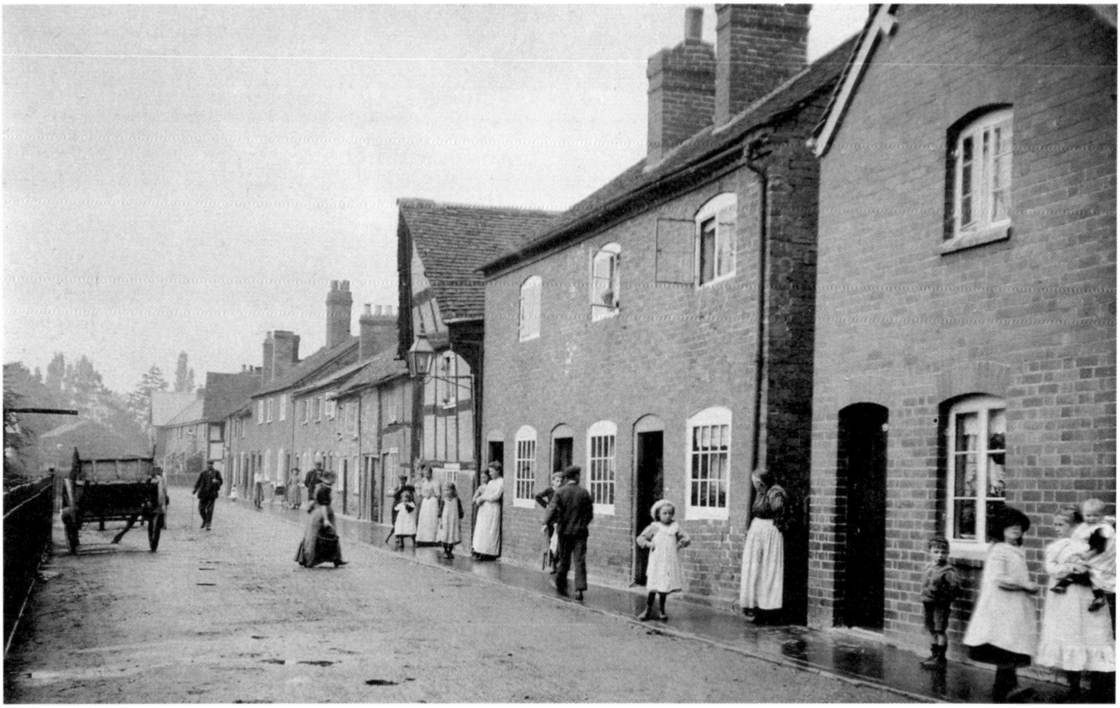

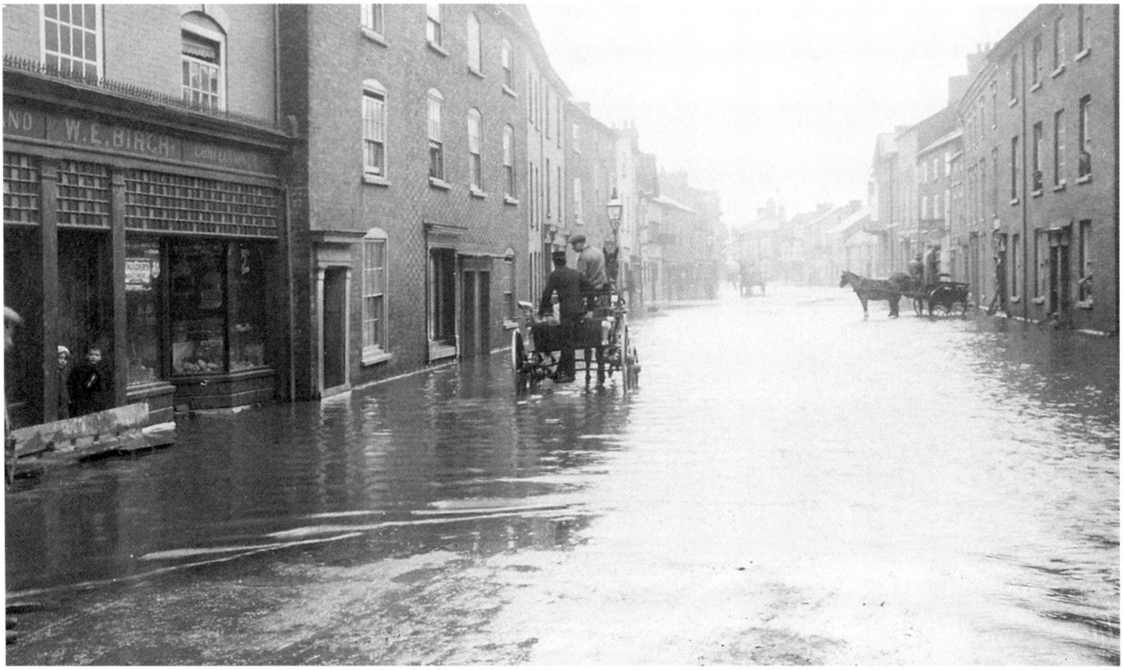

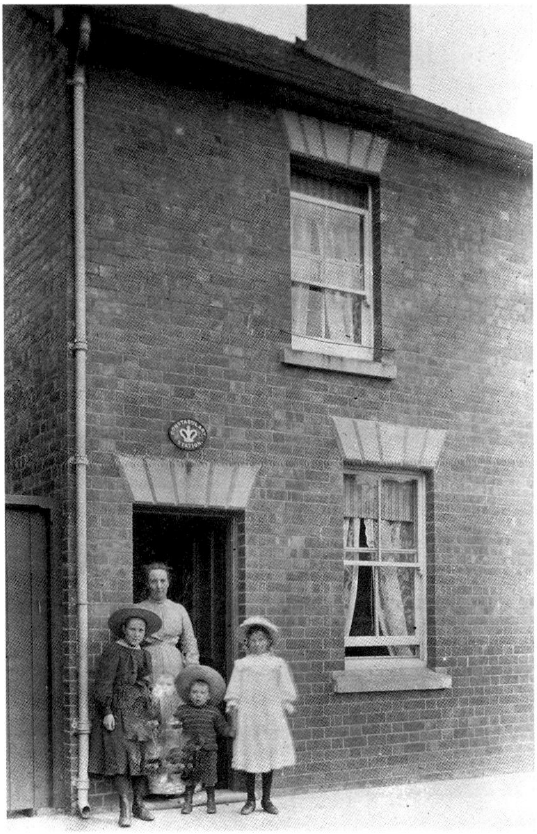

Above: *To avoid getting his feet wet, a postman hitches a lift along a flooded Bridge Street. On the left of the photograph is William Birch's bakery and confectionery shop at No.5, where his two little children gaze out at the flooded street from the safety of their doorway, well barricaded with bricks and boards against the rising flood water from the Kenwater.*

Left: *Mrs Jones, with May, Jackie and Kate Holloway, stands outside her house where the plaque over the doorway shows this was a small Constabulary Station, said to be one of the houses in Bridge Street that has since been demolished to make room for modern housing. Most of the town's police houses were, however, situated in Burgess Street near the police station.*

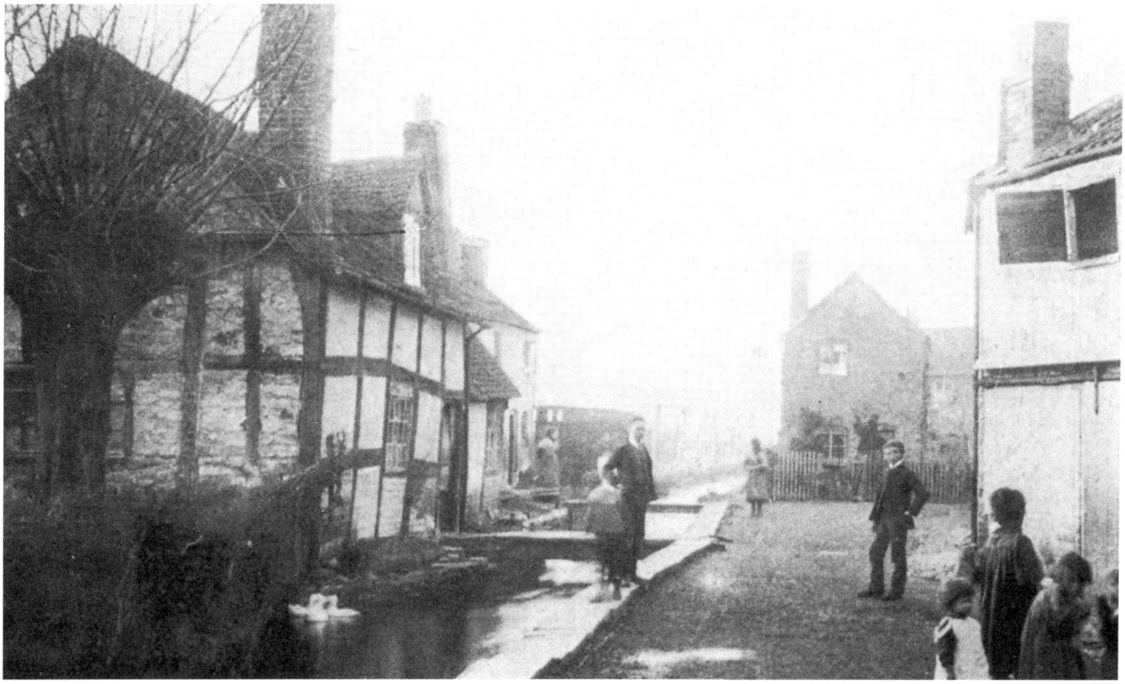

Above: *This Edwardian photograph depicts an idyllic scene where the Pinsley Brook flowed along Vicarage Street dividing some of the houses from the rest of the street. Mindful of the unknown photographer children and loungers watch a group of geese paddling in a placid eddy. Note the paved walk along the edge of the brook and several little bridges spanning the water that gave access to the houses on the 'wrong' side of the stream. It is difficult now to imagine that Vicarage Street was another area subject to flooding, since all traces of the brook were swept away in the 1960s flood prevention scheme which diverted it into the Kenwater outside the town.*

.

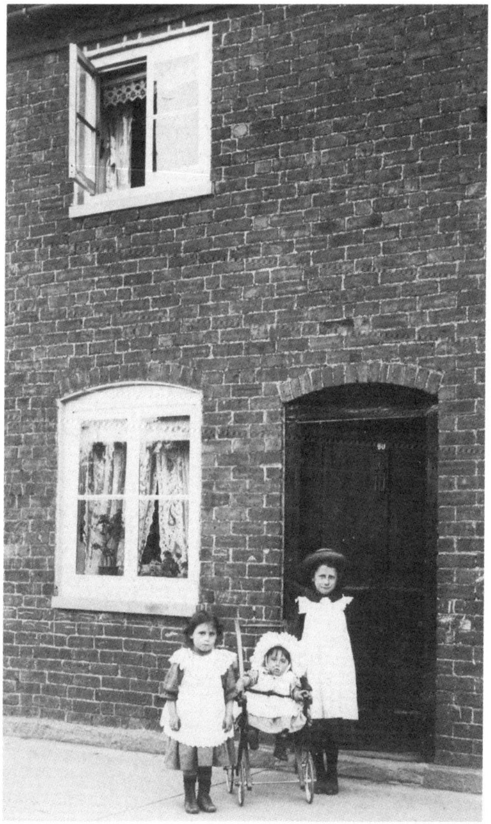

Right: *The spotlessly dressed Colley children pose outside their tiny cottage at No.20 Vicarage Street for a photograph for their family album.*

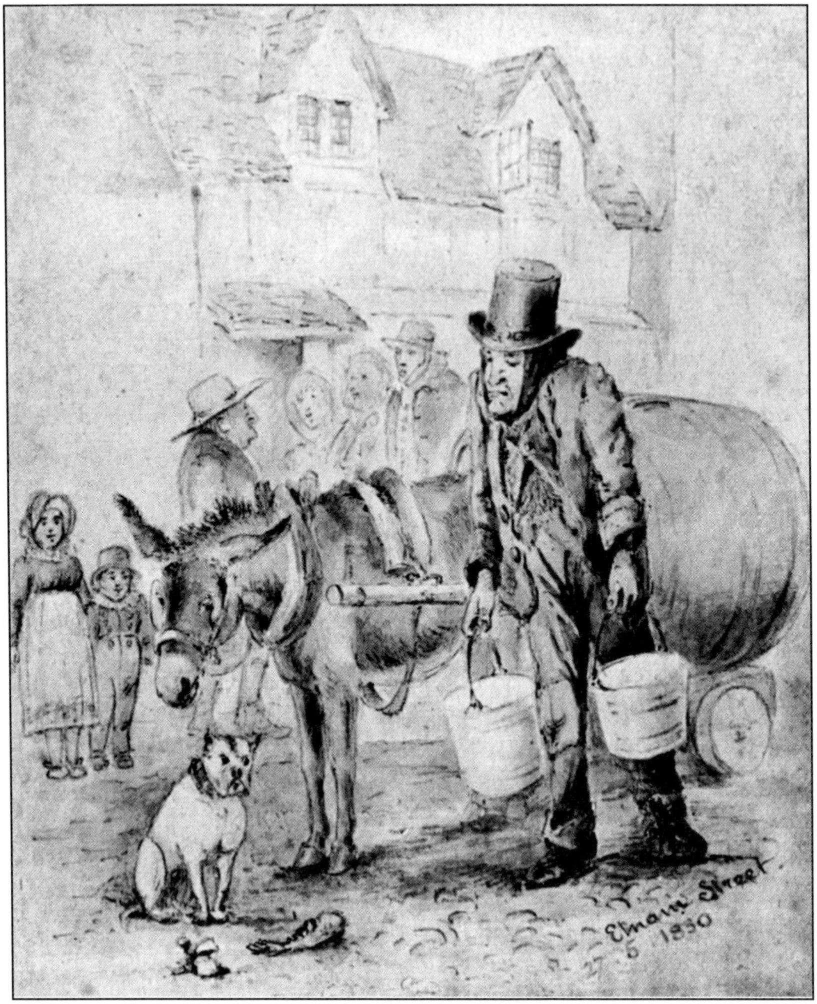

Before piped water was installed in 1867 water was obtained from shallow wells, which were liable to contamination, or bought at ½d. a bucketful from the water carrier, who dipped 'clean' water from the Lugg or Kenwater to sell to the better-off residents.

After a nationwide cholera scare, and the deaths of 38 townspeople from typhoid in 1864, the danger to health from contaminated water supplies from shallow wells and springs was finally realised. In 1867 Leominster's corporation invested £8,000 in constructing wells, a pumping station, reservoirs, and pipework for a clean water supply for the town. Water was pumped from near the railway station to two 200,000 gallon reservoirs at Newlands, each holding a day's supply. A further £5,000 was spent on a sewerage system. Soon a noticeable improvement in the health of the townspeople was noted and the systems were expanded with £5,000 spent on extending the water supply in 1900.

Broad Street

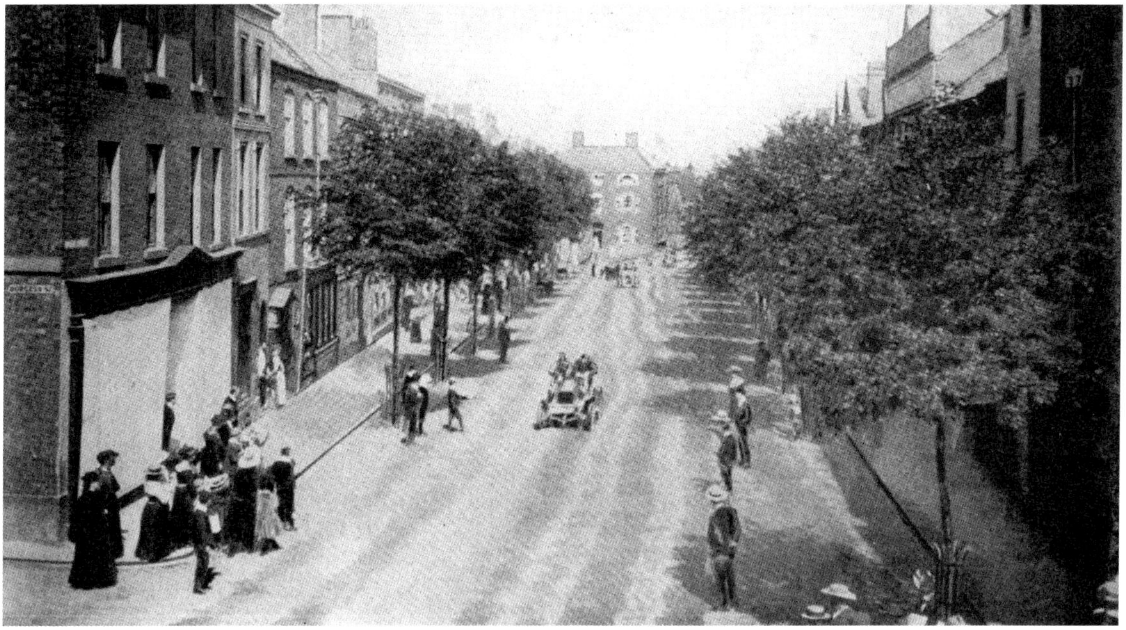

Above: *To commemorate the 1881 Herefordshire and Worcestershire Agricultural Society's show, trees costing a total of £125 were planted along Leominster's main streets. By 1906 the 25-year-old trees partially conceal the Georgian fronts of the brick and timber-framed shops of Broad Street, but together they make a pleasant background for the entrants in the 1906 rally of the Automobile Club of Great Britain and Ireland (ACGBI) on their route through Leominster. Motoring had not then become a popular pastime in Herefordshire, and only small groups of people watched the last rally organised under the auspices of the ACGBI. On 27 February 1907 King Edward VII, who was a keen motorist, commanded that the club was henceforth to be called the 'Royal Automobile Club'.*
Their performances in the rally were duly recorded in the Club's Magazine.

S. PARTRIDGE,
JEWELLER, SILVERSMITH, AND OPTICIAN,
PUBLIC LIBRARY,
BROAD STREET, LEOMINSTER.
Repairs in the various departments executed Equal to New.
ELECTRO GOODS OF EVERY DESCRIPTION RE-PLATED.
CLOCKS AND WATCHES CLEANED AND REPAIRED.
A LARGE STOCK OF FIRST-CLASS WATCHES, CLOCKS, CHAINS, FASHIONABLE JEWELLERY, JET AND IVORY ORNAMENTS, ETC.

Left: *Mr. Partridge evidently had several departments in his shop in Broad Street in 1867.*

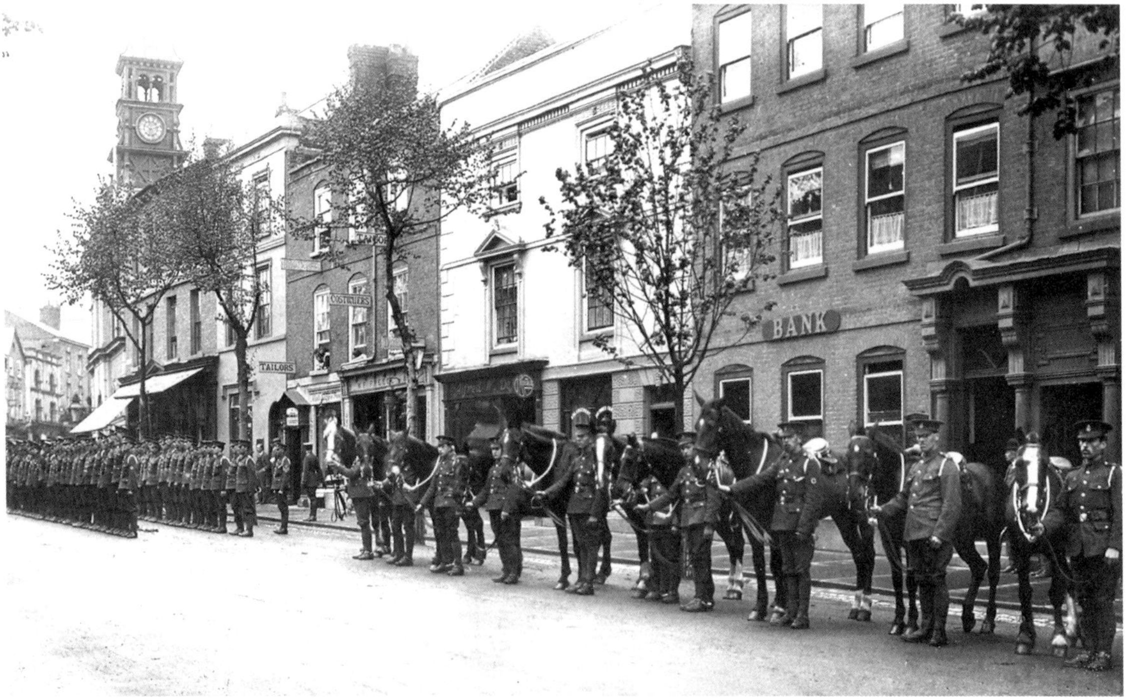

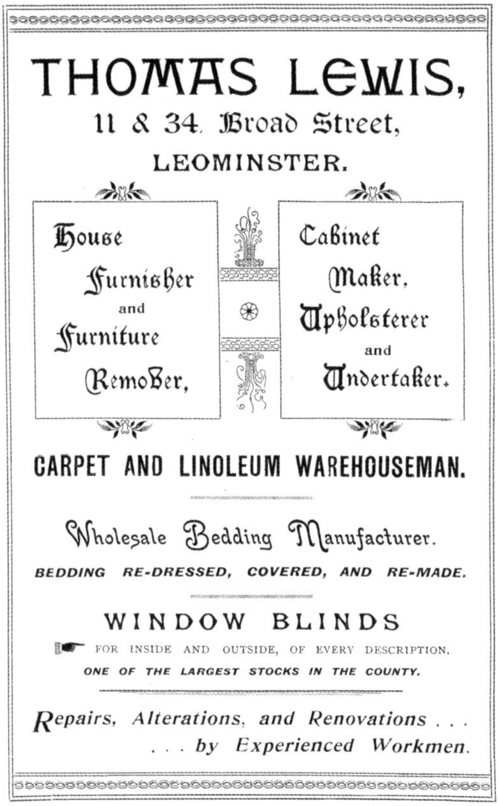

Above: *The trees gave scant shade to the parade of the horses and medics of the 14th Mounted South Wales Field Ambulance Unit who were in training in the area in 1914 before being drafted to France and Flanders.*

Starting with the Town Hall clock tower on the left, the shops on the west side of Broad Street were: at No.1, Mordant Bros., drapers, whose sun-blinds shaded the pavement; the white house, No.3, belonged to Sidney Bridge, a painter and decorator; W.F. Preece sold millinery and ladies' dresses at No.5; unsurprisingly, since he took the photograph, Alfred De'Ath's photographic shop and studio is in the centre; at No.9 the United Counties Bank, later taken over by Barclays, was managed by S.R. Taylor; and the last doorway on the extreme right opened into Thomas Lewis' long-established furniture store (see left).

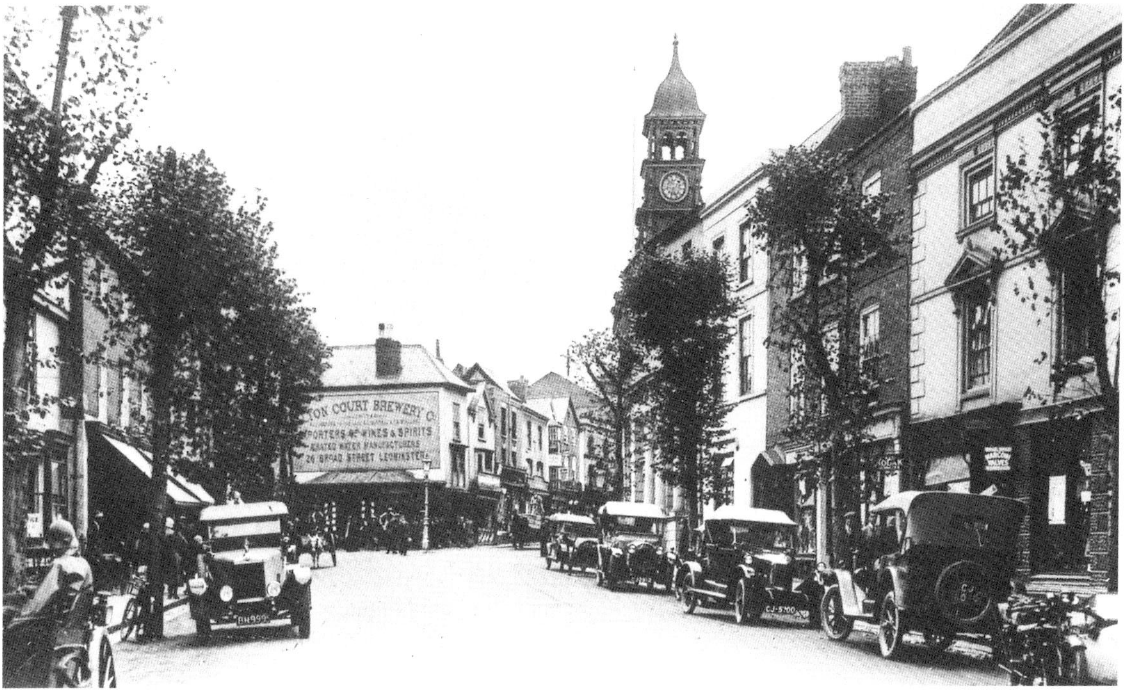

Above: *Changes in Broad Street are apparent in this 1933 photograph, taken 20 years after the one on the previous page. A sudden proliferation of cars and motor bicycles has almost taken over all the parking in the street, permanently replacing horse transport. Town officials had decided that the 50-year-old trees should be pollarded for public safety.*

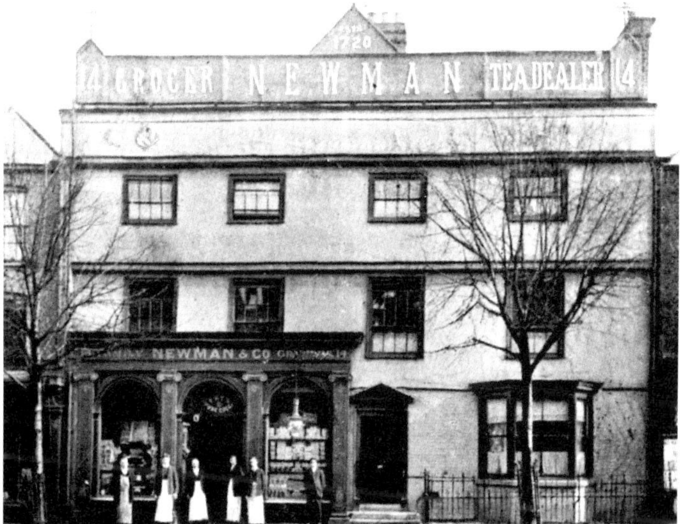

Left: *Among Broad Street's pleasant mixture of timber-framed and Georgian brick buildings, at No.14 Newman and Co. had traded in fine teas and groceries since 1720. By the Edwardian era they were wholesale and retail grocery and provision merchants and had established a branch in Llandrindod Wells 40 miles away.*

This postcard of their shop was used on an advertisement card in 1905.

Broad Street Photographers

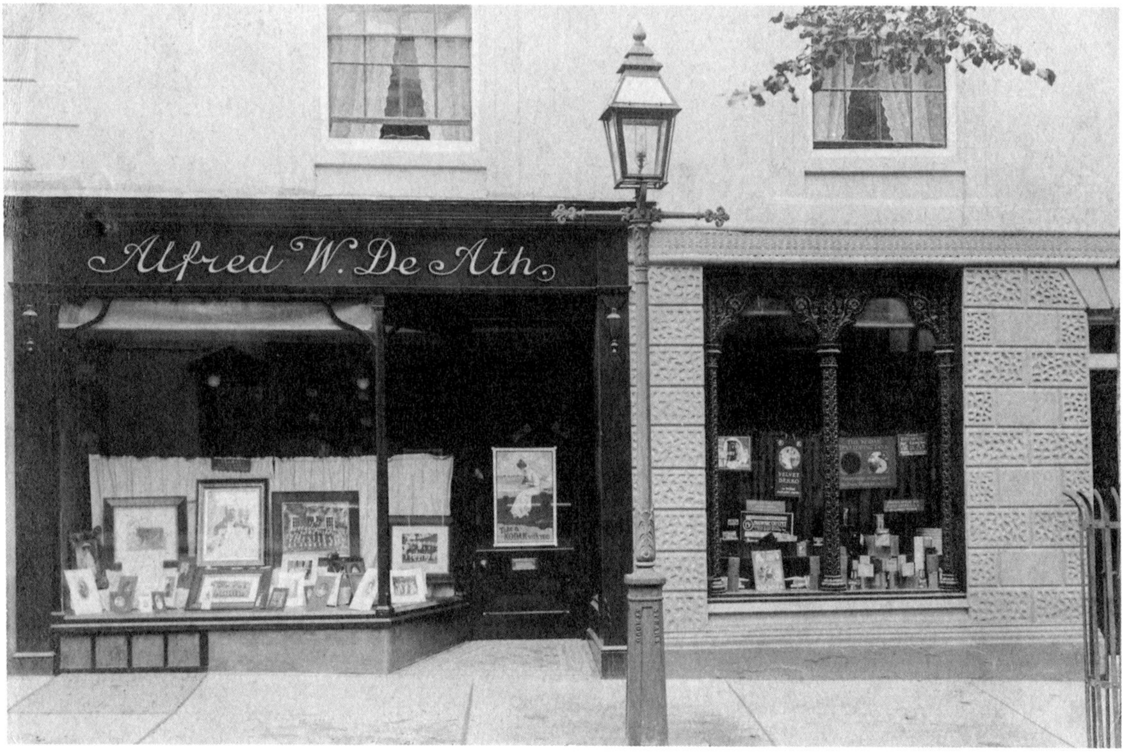

Alfred De'Ath was born in Chatham in Kent in 1873, but by 1901 he was working as a dental assistant in Leominster. By 1905, seeing the potential of a career in photography, he had taken over the studio at No.22 Burgess Street from his Baptist friend, Edward Juson Evans, on the latter's retirement. He married Margaret, a Scottish teacher, and by 1908 had moved to more prestigious premises at No.7 Broad Street, where he built a studio above a darkroom in the garden. He was a good businessman as well as a good photographer and, as his business prospered, he employed Mr Buzza as a photographic assistant. Meanwhile Margaret ran the shop and brought up their three children. Deafness prevented him from joining the army in the First World War, but it was not profound enough to stop his interest in wireless – the latest technological invention. In the next decade this developed into a large part of his business as he sold and maintained many of the early wireless sets in the area. He was a prominent Baptist and a strong supporter of the Liberal party. Tragedy struck the family when his 13-year-old son, Gordon, died from an infection after paddling in contaminated flood water. In 1930, at the age of 58, Alfred died from complications following an appendix operation. His widow was left to carry on the business with Mr Buzza's help until wartime difficulties persuaded her to retire in 1940.

Alfred sent this postcard of his new shop to his mother in Chatham in 1908.

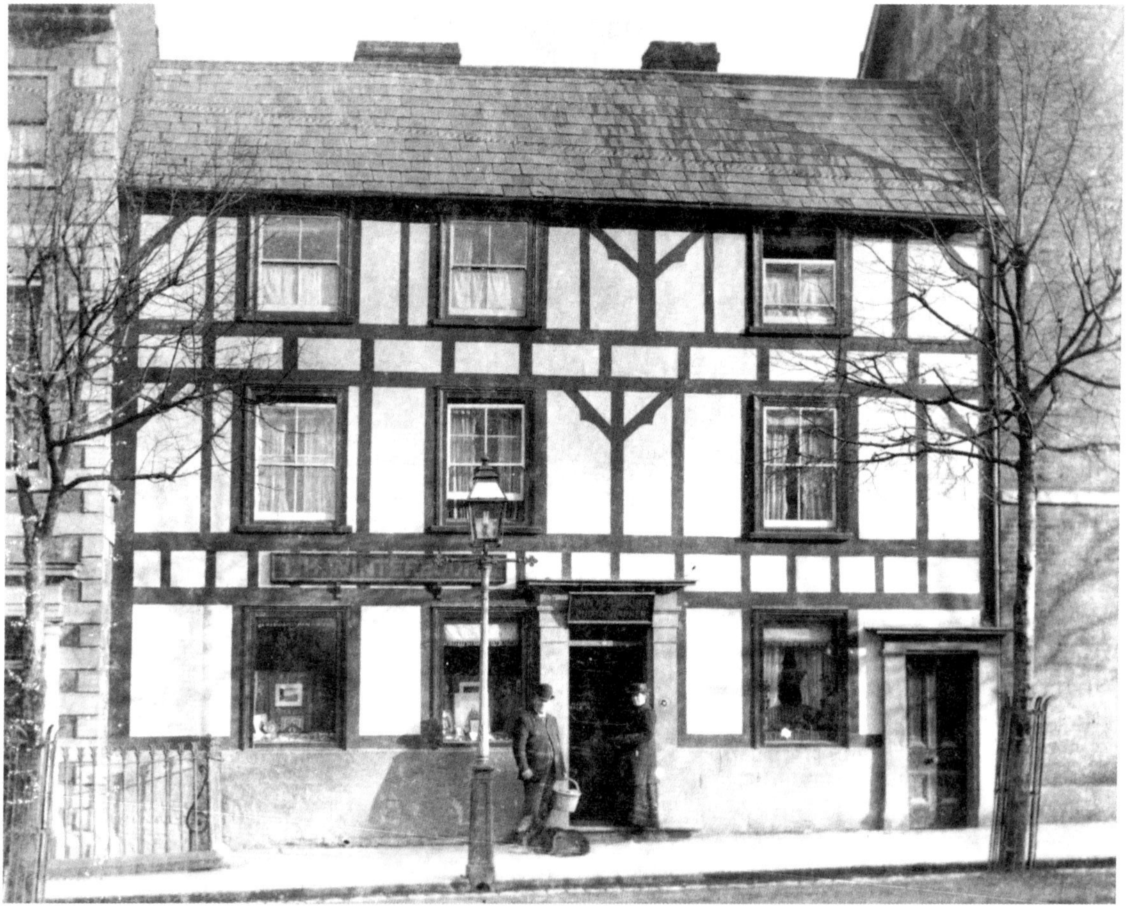

Thomas Henry Winterbourne probably settled in Leominster in the early 1870s and for a time worked for Robert Jones, whose business at No.36 Broad Street he took over in 1890. He specialised in astronomical photography, creating stereoscopic pairs of photographs which produced a three-dimensional effect when viewed through a special viewer. Membership of the Woolhope Naturalists' Field Club and parallel photographic interests led to a lasting friendship with Alfred Watkins. A man of many abilities, he lectured in physics for the extra-mural department of Oxford University and was a skilled model-maker and musician. He retired in 1911 aged about 70. His daughter, Amy, continued the business in his name until at least 1925. Winterbourne used this photograph of his shop and home in Broad Street as a Christmas card in 1904.

Alton Court Brewery Company

Alton Court Brewery Company (ACBC) of Ross expanded their successful business in the county and opened a brewery at No.26 Broad Street in Leominster in about 1900.

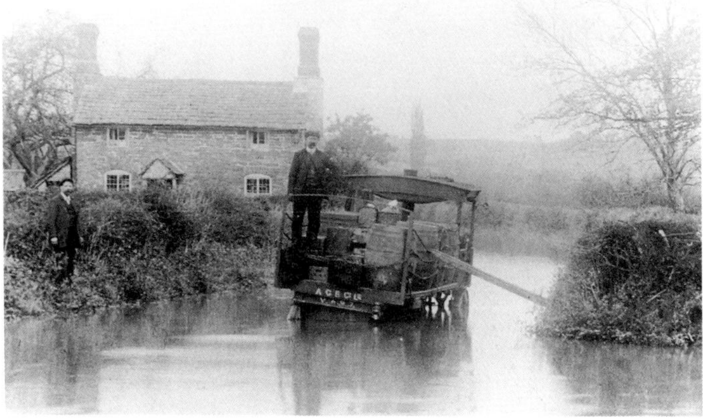

Above: *In this photograph of 1910, the ACBC steam lorry (Registration number Y692) is seen in difficulty in a flooded lane, whilst trying to deliver its load of beer.*

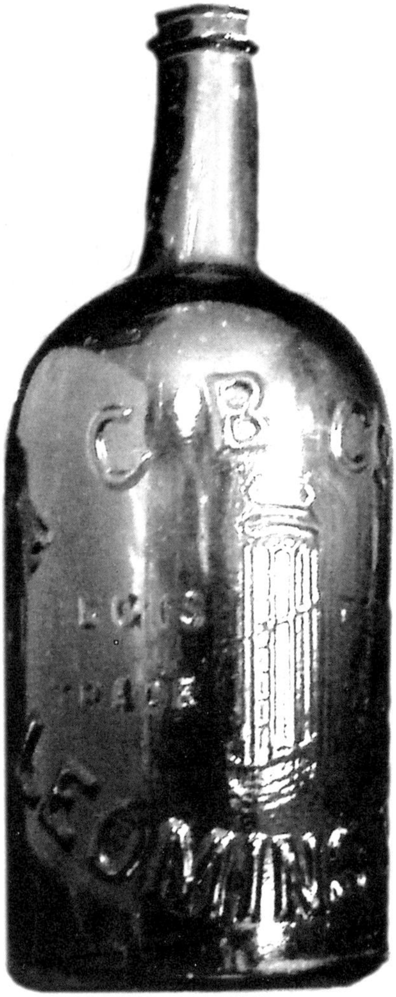

Above: *An Alton Court Brewery Company bottle.*

Right: *An 1876 advertisement for the Brewery.*

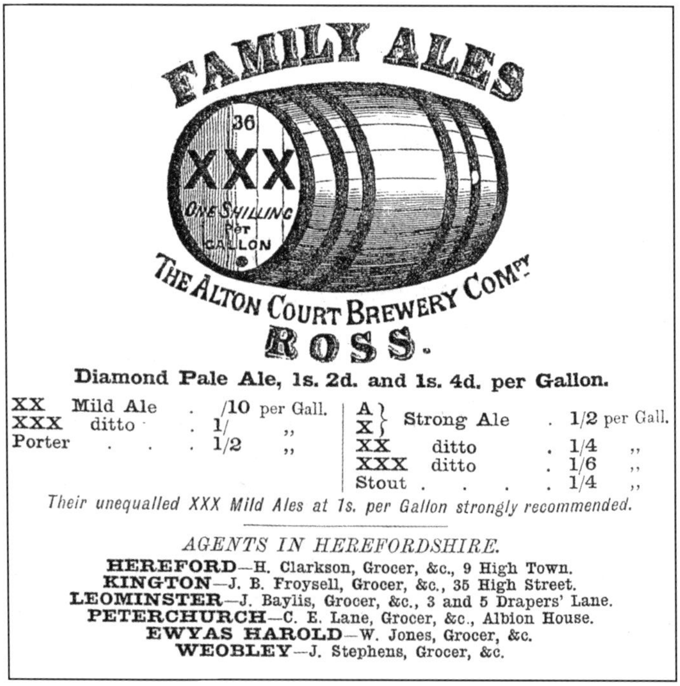

Church Street, the Town Churches and Grange Court

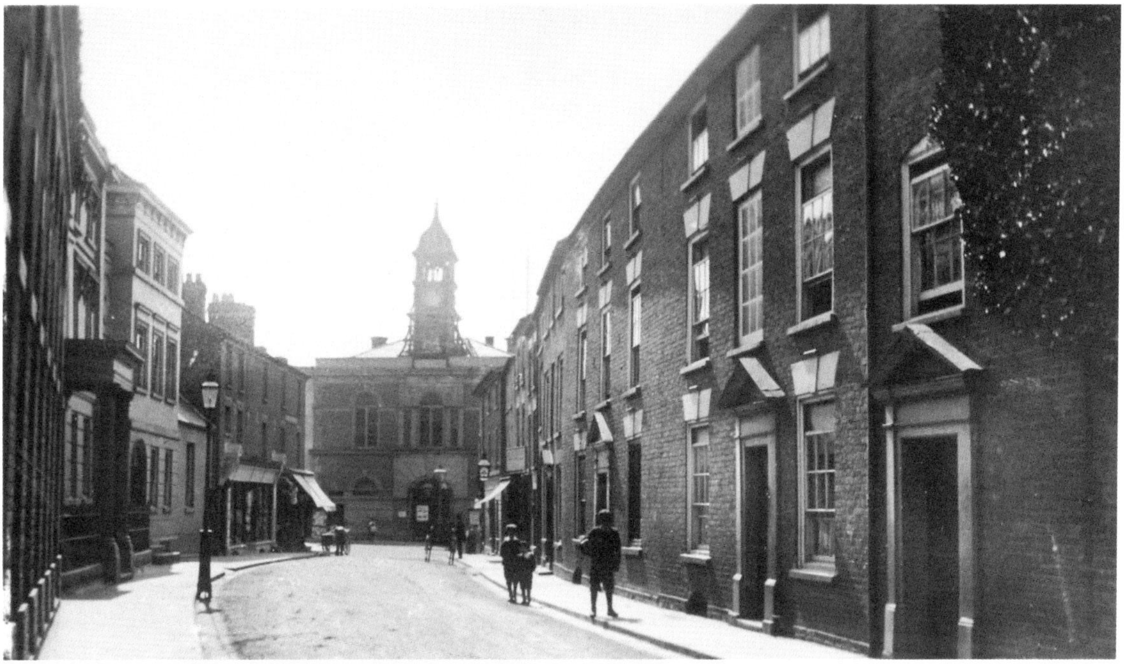

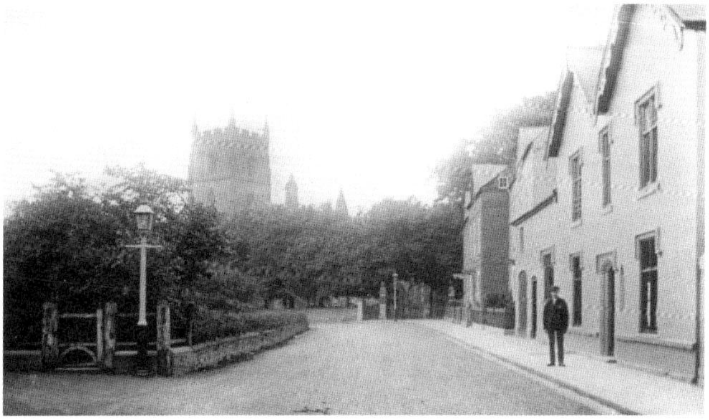

THOMAS BANNISTER,

CLOTHIER, HATTER & GENERAL OUTFITTER,

CORNER OF CHURCH STREET, LEOMINSTER,

AND

42 HIGH STREET, KINGTON.

———o———

Cloth Shooting Coats, Fancy Doe Trowsers, and Newest Styles in Vests &c. Gentlemen's Paris Hats, Boys' & Youths' Caps, Neckties, & Braces.

Above: *Apart from the disappearance in the 1960s of the Town Hall which stood in Broad Street, this view along Church Street has changed little in the hundred years since this photograph was taken. The fine Georgian façades conceal earlier buildings, hidden when it was fashionable to replace the original timber fronts with brick.*

Middle: *The gas lamp has been replaced with modern street lighting and some of the trees removed to improve the approach view of the church along this delightful Georgian street.*

Bottom: *Bannister's shop was on the corner of Church Street and High Street.*

The Priory Church

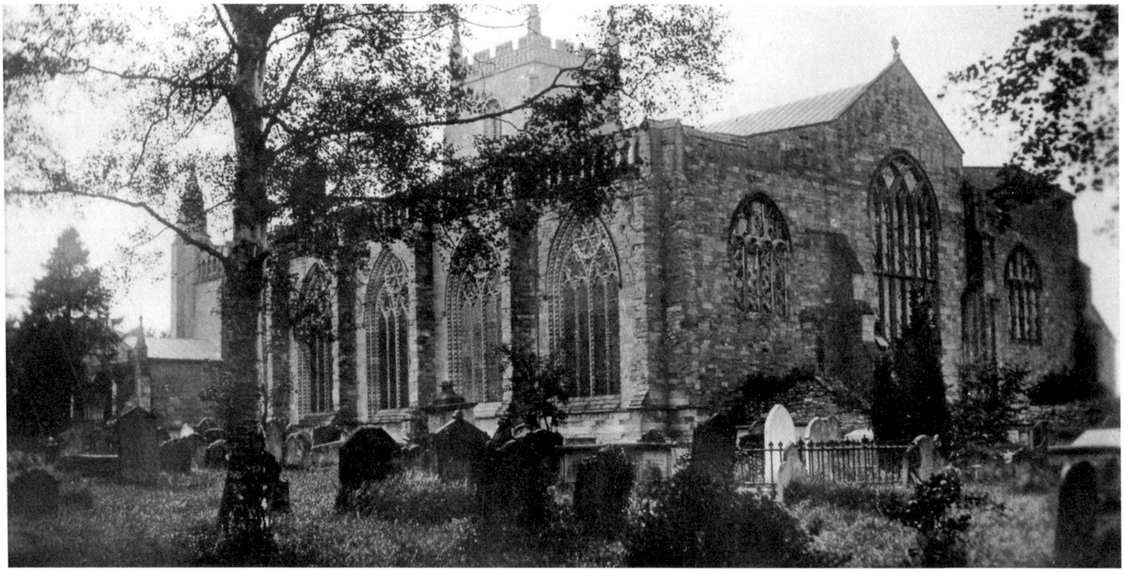

The Priory Church from the south-east in 1909 before the tombstones were removed.

Leominster's impressive Priory Church has had a varied history, having been added to and altered many times. The tower has a magnificent doorway, carved with figures typical of the Herefordshire School of Romanesque Sculpture. There is impressive Norman stonework in the north wall of the nave; a Perpendicular window in the central nave and Early Decorated windows in the south wall. Dedicated to Saints Peter and Paul, the church possesses early silver-ware and registers dating back to 1549, together with other important account books. The wool trade fluctuated at different periods in Leominster's history and the church reflects the wealth derived from the centuries when wool trading was very profitable, both for the church and the town.

Appalled at the neglect he found when he arrived in 1862, the new vicar, the Revd A.G. Edouart entrusted Sir George Gilbert Scott, whose work in restoring churches was well known, with the task of restoring the building, little dreaming that the huge task would take nearly 30 years of intermittent work. The first priority was the restoration of the imposing Norman nave which was completed in 1866 at a cost of £3,012. It took another 13 years before the central part of the nave and the Early English south porch were rebuilt. After £1,200 had been spent on works to the tower, the fabric restoration was completed in 1891. Finally, in 1894, the original peal of eight bells was re-hung together with two new ones at a cost of £354.

The Revd Edouart must have thought the total cost of over £12,000, much of it raised from private donations, to be money well spent. The completion coincided with a religious revival that led to bigger congregations listening to the sermons of this popular vicar, whose incumbency came to an end in 1896 after 34 years.

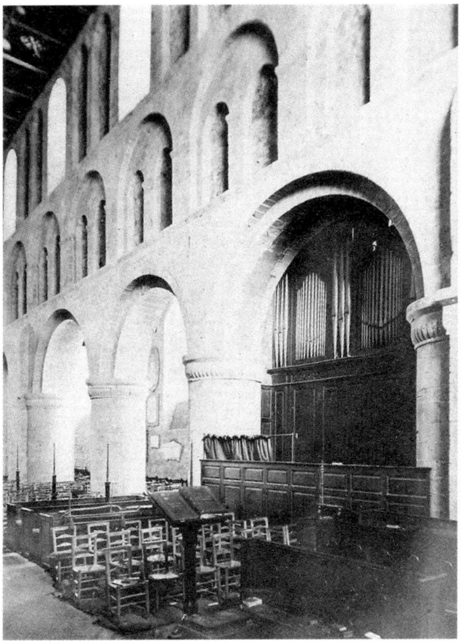

Left: *This photograph, on a* carte de visite, *was produced by Robert Jones some time between 1870 and 1878. Wooden chairs fill the nave, replacing the old wooden box pews. The old organ, dating from 1737, was repaired in 1797 and again in 1842. It occupied at least four different positions in the church until it finally broke down irretrievably in 1921.*

Below: *For ten years an American harmonium was used until a new organ could be installed. Fortunately the need for a replacement organ had been foreseen in 1911 and a fund had been started. However, due to the disruption caused by the war years, it had only grown to £400. Under the spirited guidance of the new secretary, William Drennan, who was the Grammar School headmaster, local appeals increased the fund to £1,700. A former church choirboy, Stanley Holland, then living in Chicago, heard of the problem and came to the rescue with the funds needed. Installation was carried out by the Worcester firm of Nicholson and Co. under the direction of Professor. J. Bridge. The new organ was dedicated just a week before Christmas 1924.*

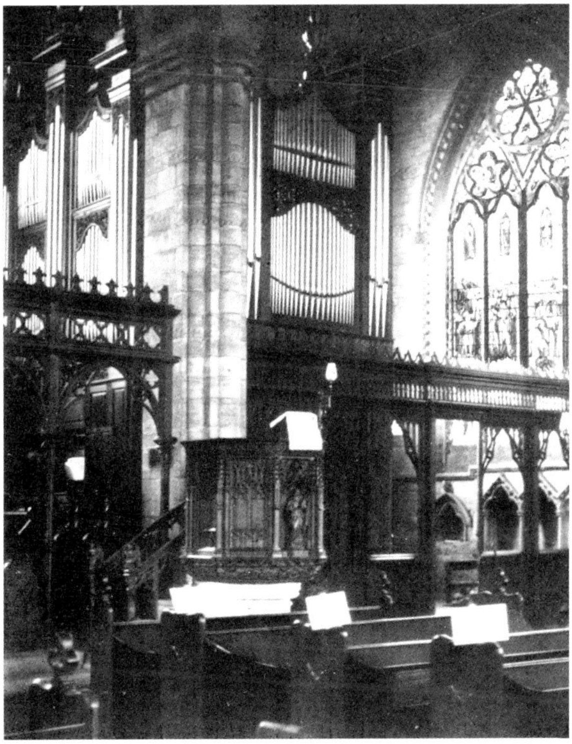

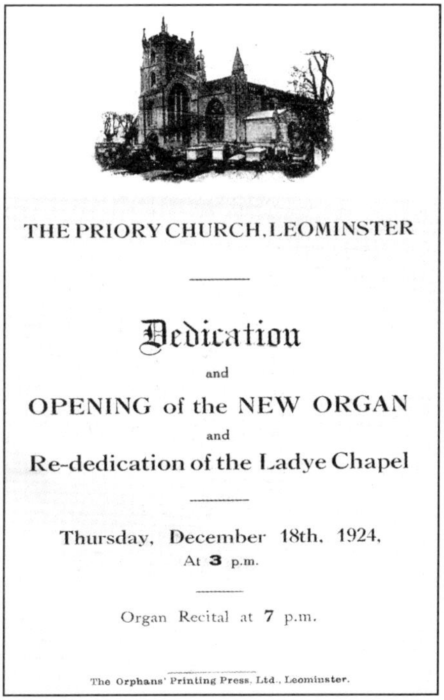

THE PRIORY CHURCH, LEOMINSTER

Dedication

and

OPENING of the NEW ORGAN

and

Re-dedication of the Ladye Chapel

Thursday, December 18th, 1924,

At 3 p.m.

Organ Recital at 7 p.m.

The Orphans' Printing Press, Ltd., Leominster.

Left and above: *Dedication of the new organ.*

The Ducking Stool

Until 1809 Leominster's ducking stool had occasionally been used as a punishment for tradesmen who sold either underweight or adulterated goods; and to quieten loud-mouthed women. On some of these unfortunate ladies this punishment had the opposite effect.

Right: *Cracked and repaired, the stool has been kept in safety in the north aisle of the Priory Church since about 1895. Previously it had been stored in the old Borough Gaol at No.23 New Street, until the Herefordshire Volunteers took over the building for use as a drill hall.*

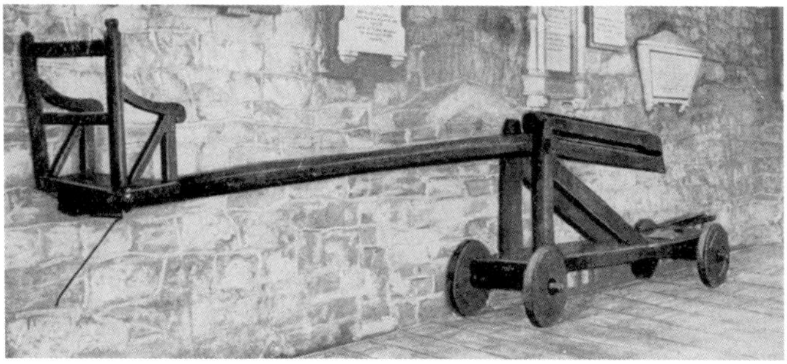

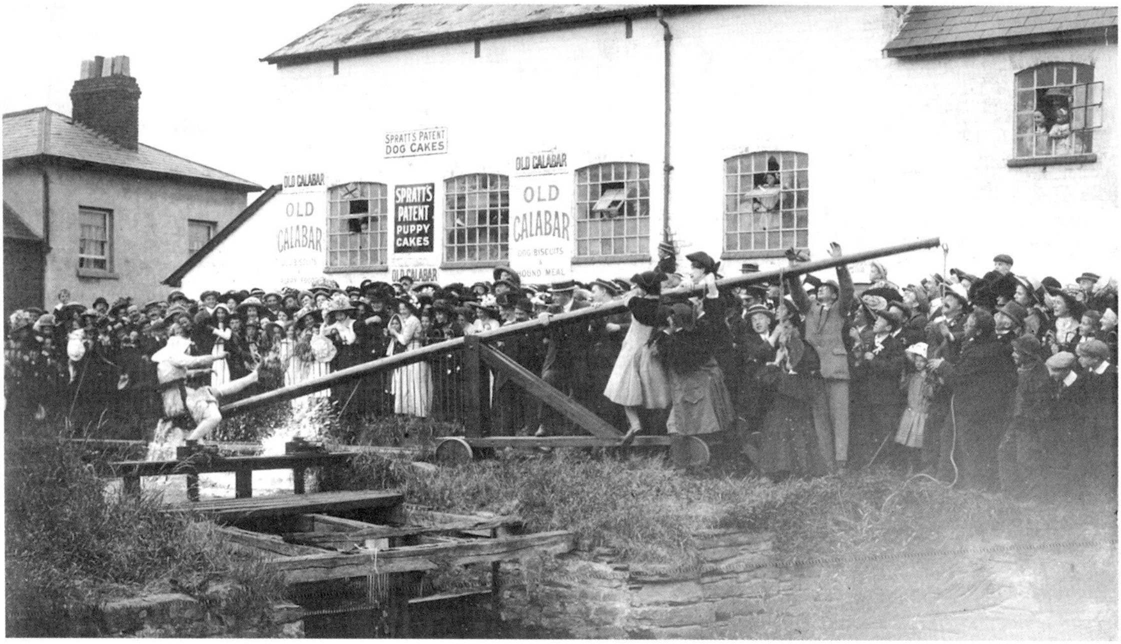

Above: *To prevent damage to the original, a replica of the ducking stool was built and positioned beside Porter's Mill in Mill Street for a carnival in about 1914. The intention was both to raise money and to demonstrate its former use. Comparing it with the original shows that the wheels of the replica were smaller and the seat was of a different design. In a happy reversal of roles a group of women, joyfully encouraged by their sisters in the crowd and at the windows of the mill, enthusiastically applaud the ducking of the unfortunate male volunteer in the mill pool. The vehicle entrance to Paradise Court now covers all this site; only the house on the left in Mill Street remains.*

St Ethelbert's Roman Catholic Church

St. Ethelbert's Roman Catholic Church in Bargates opened in May 1888, replacing a smaller church in Burgess Street, which the congregation had used for the previous 20 years. Mrs. Herbert, widow of a former Mayor, met the £2,300 cost of the new church, which was designed by P.P. Pugin to seat 200 worshippers. An unusual feature is that, due to the cramped site available, the church could not be built on the usual east-west alignment.

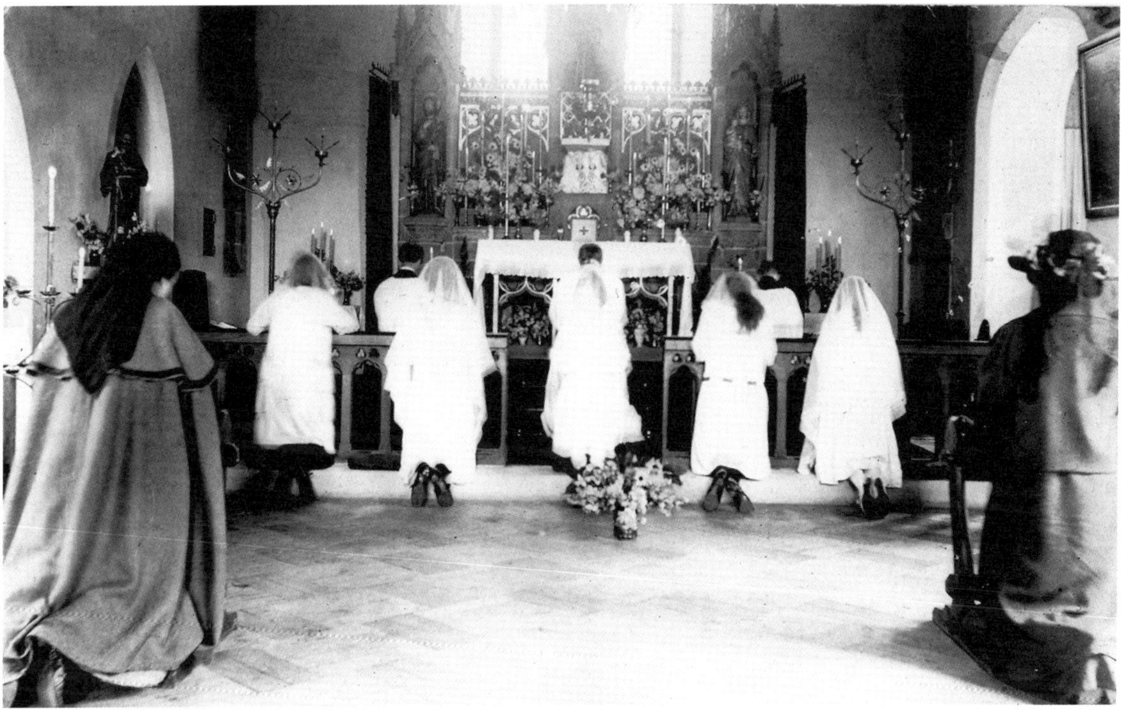

Photographs of religious services are scarce, but this one was taken during the celebration of a mass at which some of the congregation were to receive the blessed sacrament for the first time. The priest, Father Roberts, is in the centre facing the altar and behind him five girls, wearing the white dresses and white veils that are customary at this important event in their spiritual life, have left the posies that they had been carrying on the floor and kneel at the altar-rail waiting to make their first communion.

The Old Town Hall – Grange Court

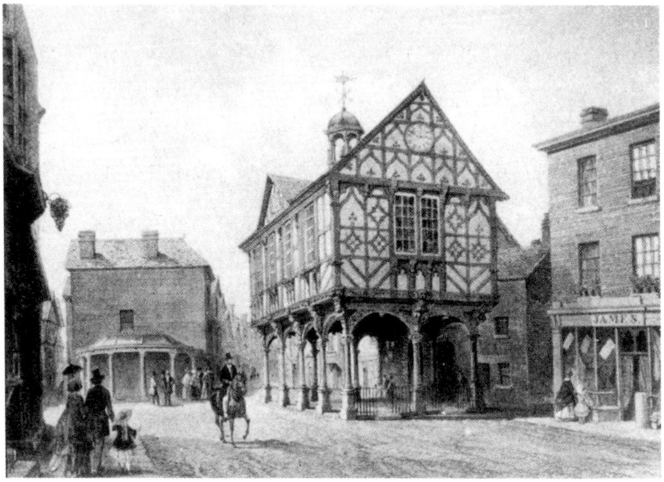

Top: *The old Town Hall when it was at the top of Broad Street.*

In 1853 John Arkwright of Hampton Court bought the Town Hall for £95. When it was built in 1633 it reflected the wealth and power of the local merchant guilds. However, by 1850 it had become an obstacle to the free flow of the increasing number of vehicles wanting to drive through the town centre.

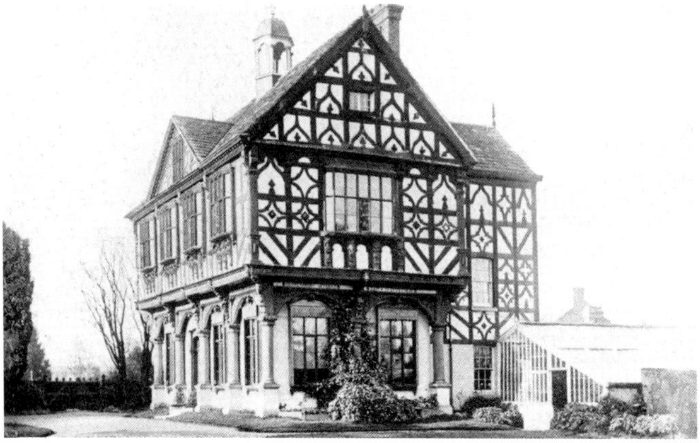

Middle: *After considerable debate with the Town Elders over its future, Arkwright had it moved to one of his plots of land at the Grange. There, it was re-erected and, with the ground floor enclosed and a rear extension, it took on a second life as a private house. Arkwright leased it to a Leominster solicitor, providing extra income for his dwindling estate funds.*

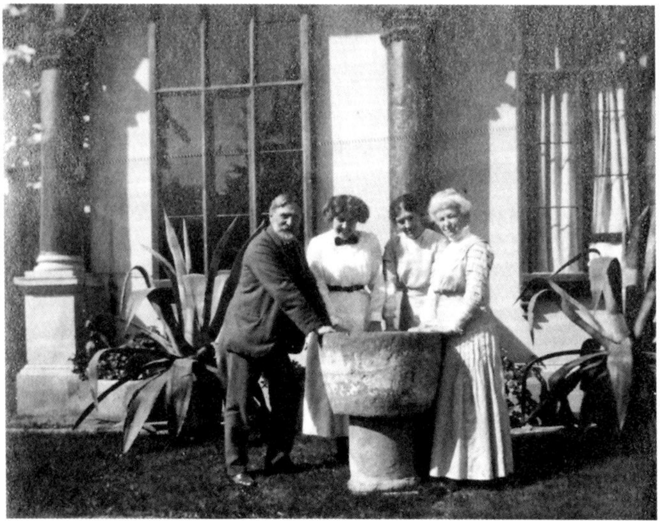

Bottom: *In 1907 his son, Jack Arkwright, was forced to auction the estate's town properties to pay death duties. Theodore Neild, J.P., a prominent local Quaker, bought the house privately and after some necessary renovations, settled there for many years.*

In 1910 he used this photograph of their happy family group enjoying their new garden as their Christmas card.

High Street, Drapers Lane and Victoria Street

Broad Street suddenly narrows into High Street as it continues through Leominster town centre with small connecting streets leading to Corn Square. Built for horse-drawn traffic it became a serious traffic bottleneck in the mid-twentieth century until the ring road and the A49 bypass were built, relieving the town centre of the increasing traffic congestion.

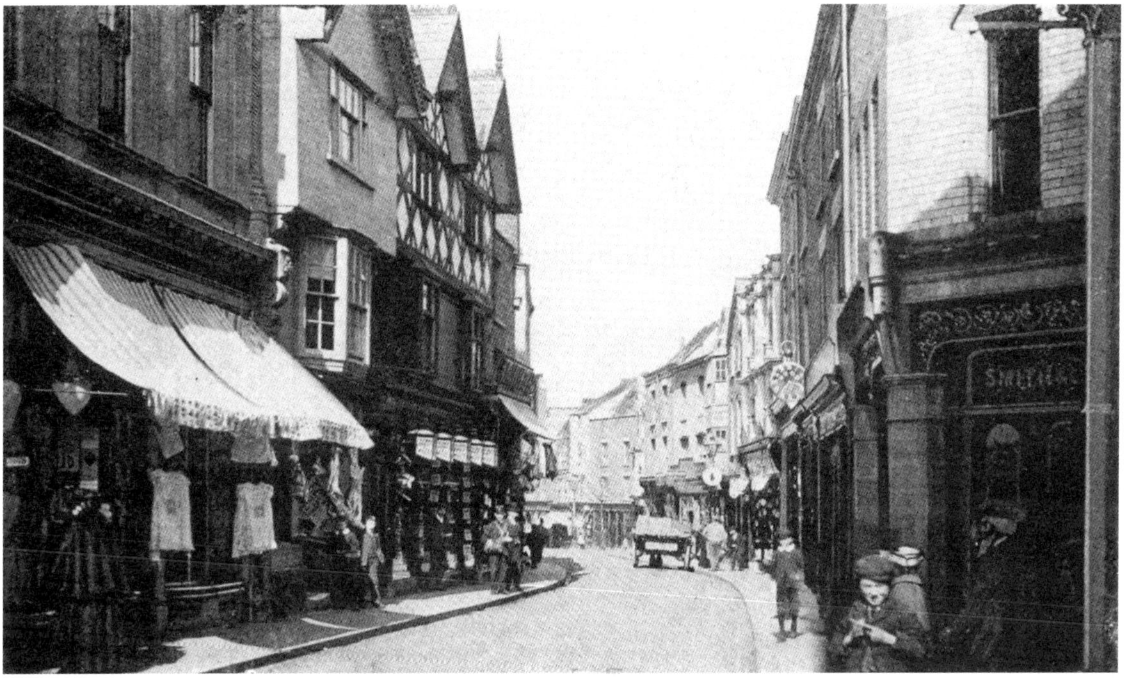

High Street facing north in the early 1900s showing the timber-framed buildings in a variety of styles and dates. The Victorian fashion for plaster rendering has hidden some of their timbers, giving them a plain appearance beside the fine exposed timbers of their neighbours.

MARGARET DAVIS,

Candle Manufactory,

Warehouse for Composites, Soaps, Blue, Starch, Soda, Burning Oils, Brushes, Brooms, &c.,

WHOLESALE AND RETAIL,

32 High Street, LEOMINSTER.

Families in the Country are supplied on the most liberal Terms.

Candle and soap making were two of the many trades that were taking place in the centre of Leominster at the end of the 19th century.

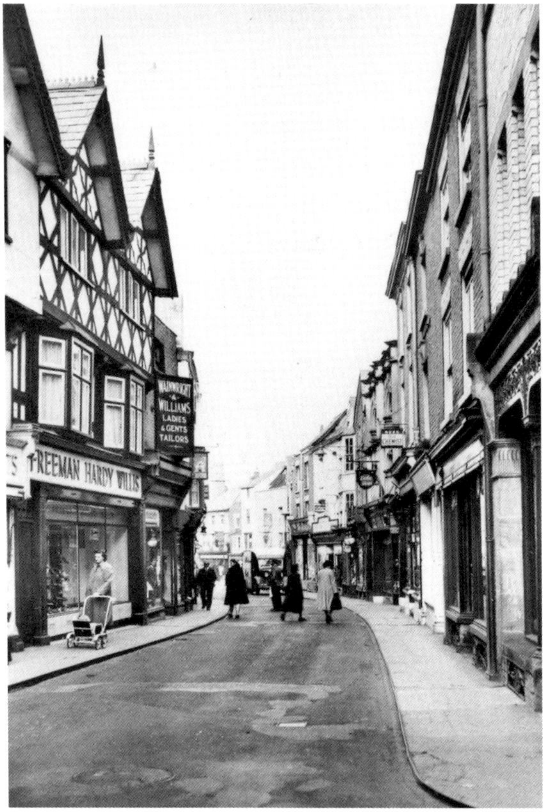

Left: *High Street was at the hub of Leominster, with two-way traffic on the busy A49 road. Towards the end of the 19th century it had a wide variety of shops; at the northern end of the street, at the corner with Burgess Street, was the Town Hall which faced onto Church Street. High Street continued southwards to the Iron Cross (as the junction with West Street is called) and a little further to the south, Etnam Street joined the north/south road from the east. Here the A49 changed its name once again, becoming, appropriately, South Street.*

Below: *Eastman's were a chain of butchers with branches in Ledbury and Hereford as well as their Leominster shop at No.45 High Street. Before regulations on food hygiene were enforced butchers habitually put the carcasses of their butchered animals and birds on display to attract customers.*

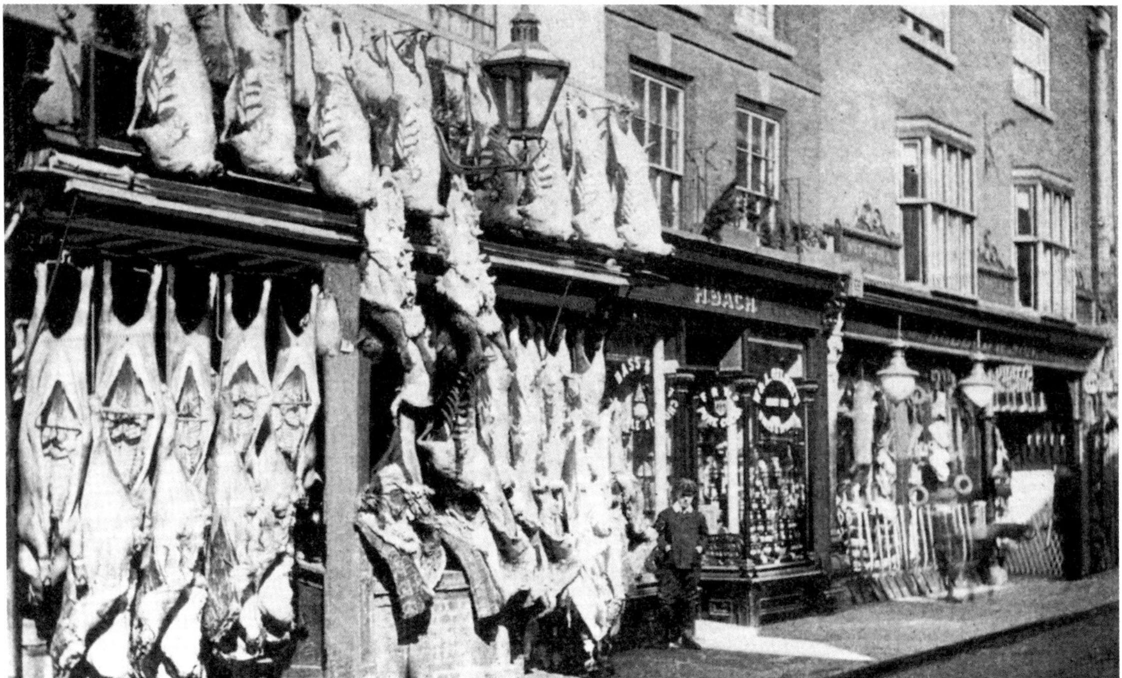

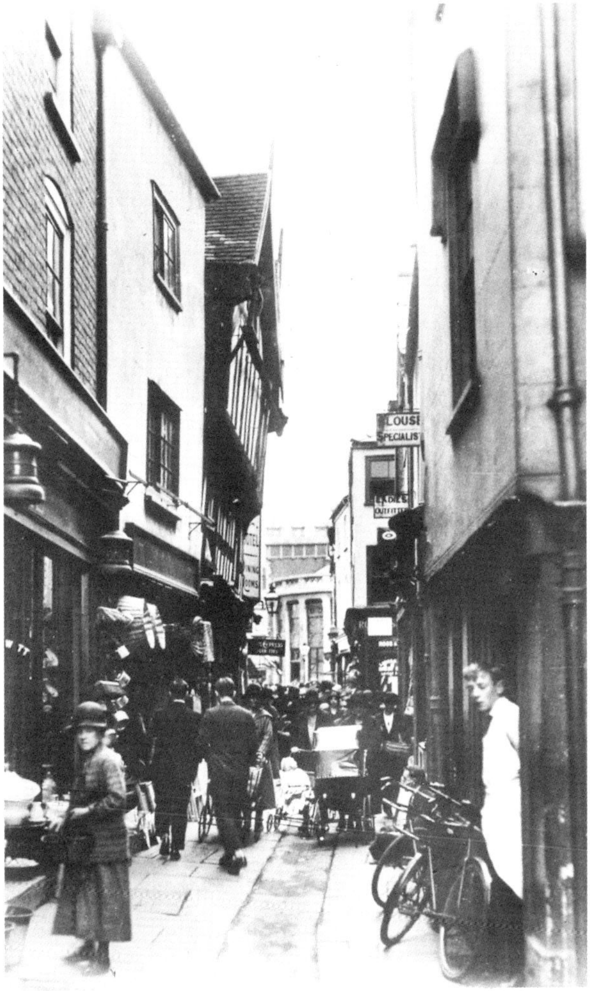

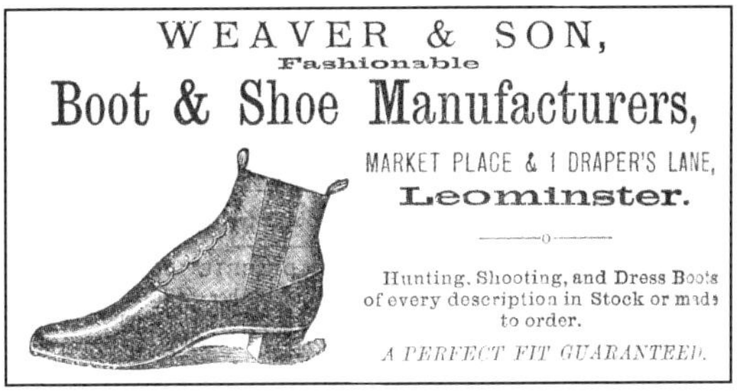

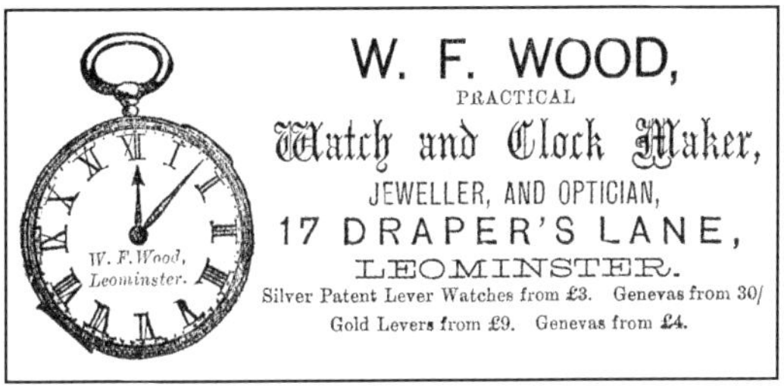

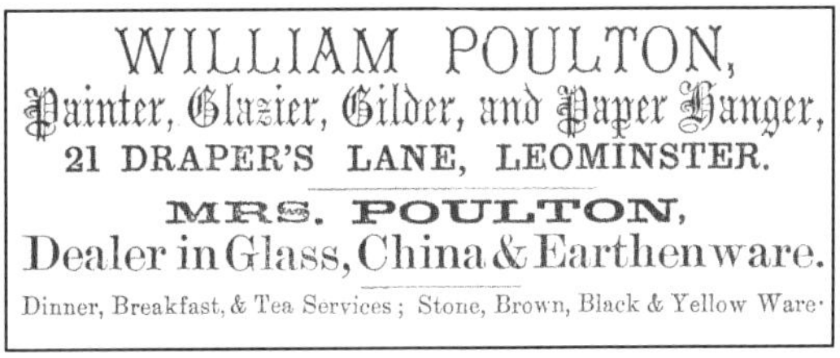

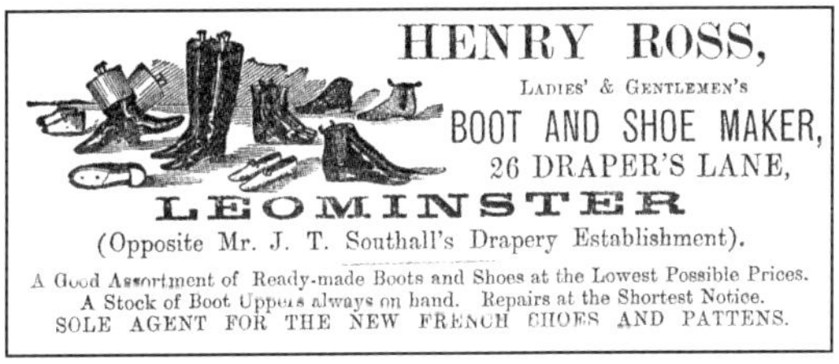

The medieval origin and character of Drapers Lane, the ever-busy thoroughfare that connects Broad Street and Corn Square, is revealed in the projecting upper floors – a typical construction of timber-framed houses. Since this 1920s photograph was taken, the appearance of the shops has not changed – it is only the owners that are different. On the left, Mary Hewitt ran the glass, china and hardware shop at Nos.3, 5, and 7 for over two decades. Opposite, at No.2, Gough's delivery boy steals a glance at Lilywhite's photographer before starting on his next delivery round. This shop later became the Leominster News *office and is now the local Tourist Information Office. Note the unusual gas-lamp over Mary Hewitt's shop.*

The advertisements on the right give an impression of the wide variety of trades and professions in this short, narrow street at the beginning of the 20th century.

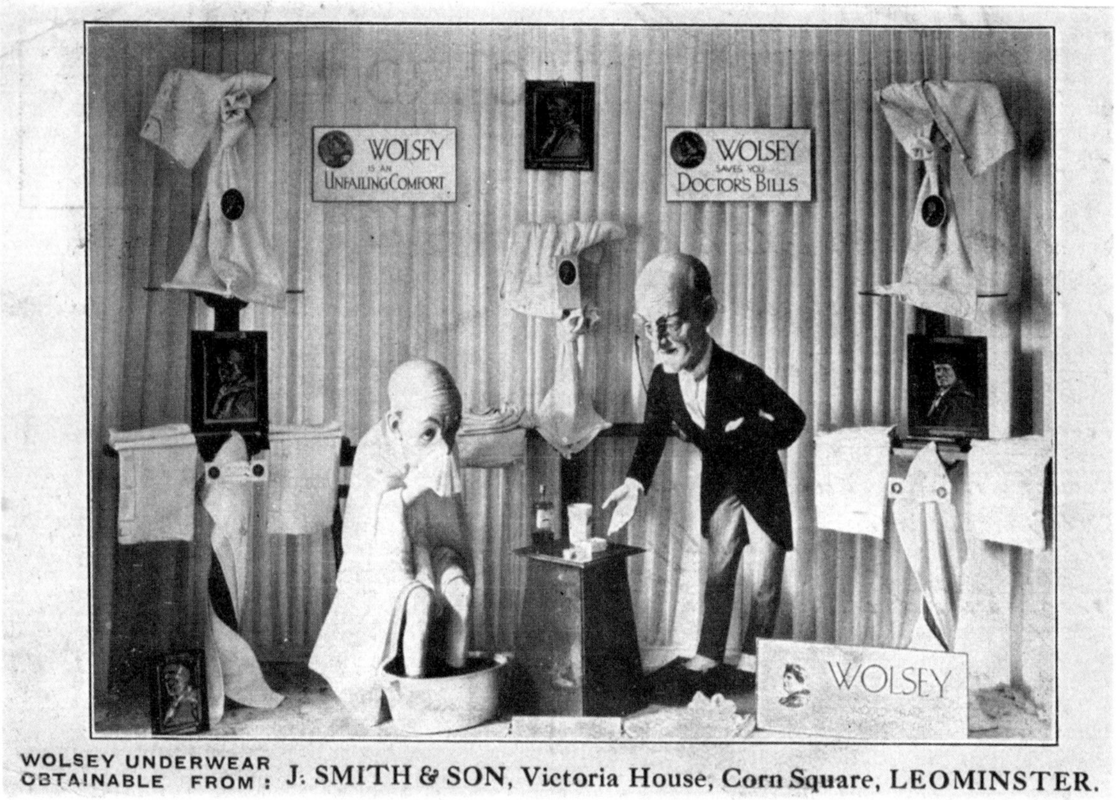

J. Smith and Son made use of a Wolsey advertising postcard to promote their millinery, clothing and carpet shop, at Victoria House, Nos.5 and 7 Victoria Street. This short street, which joins High Street to Drapers Lane, was constructed in 1885 to improve the access to Corn Square.

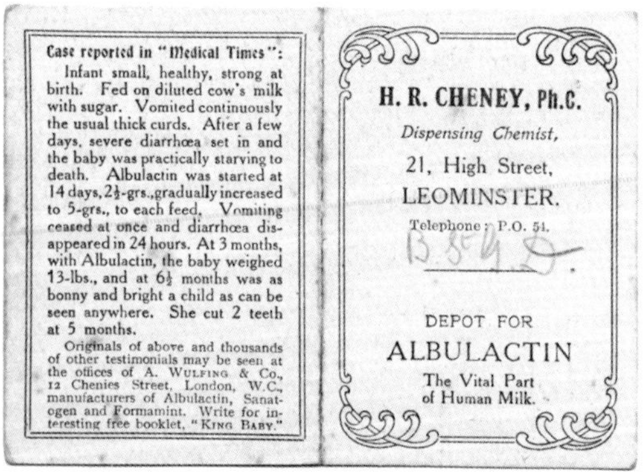

Case reported in "Medical Times":

Infant small, healthy, strong at birth. Fed on diluted cow's milk with sugar. Vomited continuously the usual thick curds. After a few days, severe diarrhœa set in and the baby was practically starving to death. Albulactin was started at 14 days, 2½-grs., gradually increased to 5-grs., to each feed. Vomiting ceased at once and diarrhœa disappeared in 24 hours. At 3 months, with Albulactin, the baby weighed 13-lbs., and at 6½ months was as bonny and bright a child as can be seen anywhere. She cut 2 teeth at 5 months.

Originals of above and thousands of other testimonials may be seen at the offices of A. WULFING & Co., 12 Chenies Street, London, W.C., manufacturers of Albulactin, Sanatogen and Formamint. Write for interesting free booklet, "KING BABY."

H. R. CHENEY, Ph.C.
Dispensing Chemist,
21, High Street,
LEOMINSTER.
Telephone: P.O. 51.

DEPOT FOR
ALBULACTIN
The Vital Part
of Human Milk.

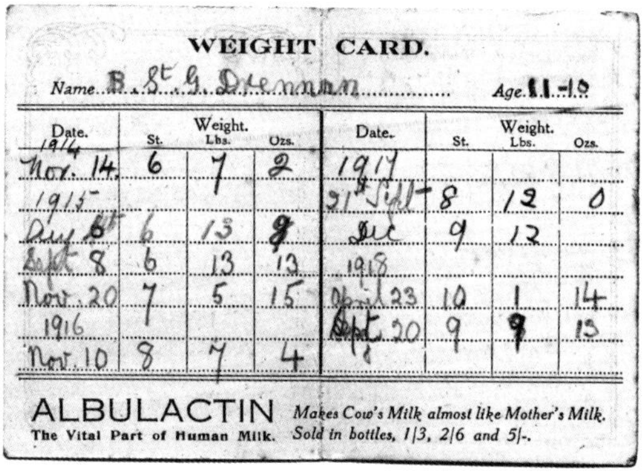

WEIGHT CARD.

Name [illegible] Age 11-10

Date.	Weight. St.	Lbs.	Ozs.	Date.	Weight. St.	Lbs.	Ozs.
1914 Nov. 14	6	7	2	1917			
1915				21st Sept	8	12	0
Aug 6th	6	13	9	Dec	9	12	
Sept 8	6	13	13	1918			
Nov. 20	7	5	15	April 23	10	1	14
1916				Sept 20	9	9	13
Nov. 10	8	7	4				

ALBULACTIN
The Vital Part of Human Milk.
Makes Cow's Milk almost like Mother's Milk. Sold in bottles, 1/3, 2/6 and 5/-.

Henry Robert Cheney, pharmaceutical chemist, was listed in Kelly's 1909 and 1922 Directories. *His shop and dispensary at No.21 High Street stocked all the latest remedies, medicines and baby foods needed by a generation of Leominster townspeople. Customers' babies and children were all given this advertisement weight card to chart their growth.*

Corn Square

Connected by Victoria Street and Corn Street to High Street lies the large open area of Corn Square, which for centuries has been Leominster's market and meeting place and, except on market days, now serves the town as a car park. On its south side the narrow pedestrianised School Lane leads past specialist shops to Etnam Street. Grange Lane leads east to the Grange. Overlooked by shops in Leominster's usual mixture of architectural styles, the Square has seen preachers, politicians, union leaders and others deliver their special message to the townsfolk, who really preferred to turn up in numbers for a bit of fun at carnivals, parades, proclamations and the like.

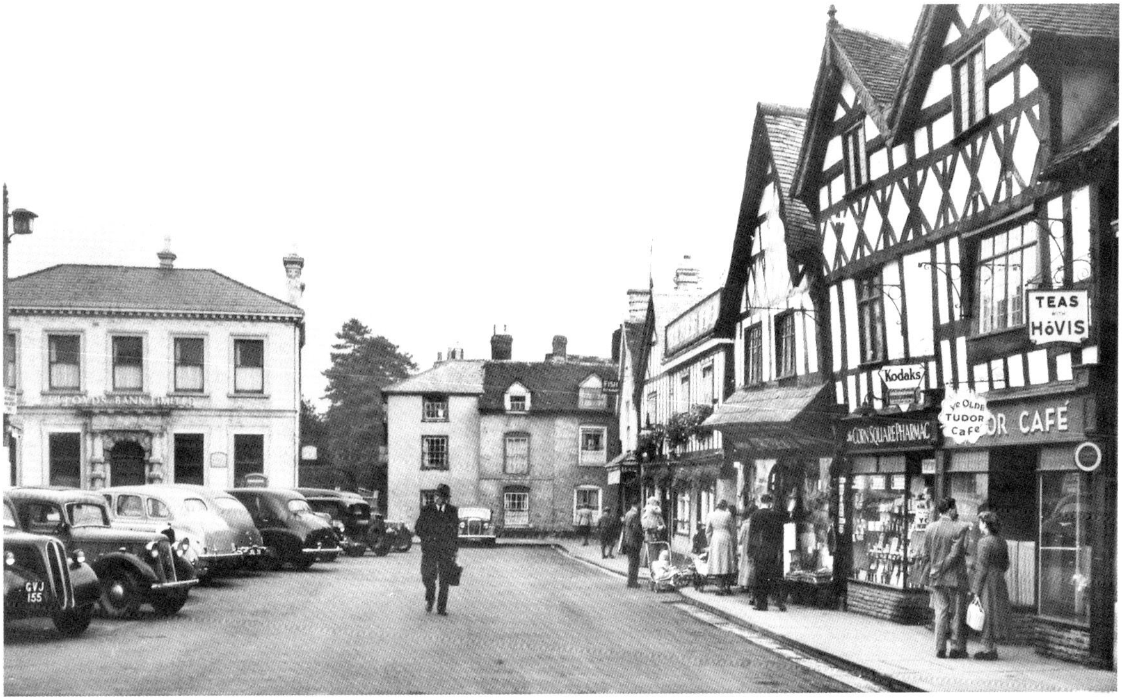

Looking east in Corn Square. Older inhabitants speak highly of the teas served in the Tudor Café in the 1940s and 50s; next door was the Leominster Pharmacy. Last in the row of timbered shops was a popular clothes emporium extending along School Lane. In the centre of the photograph the dull Victorian plaster covering the old timbers of the Merchant's House on the corner of Grange Lane has since been removed, giving that corner of the square a much more attractive appearance.

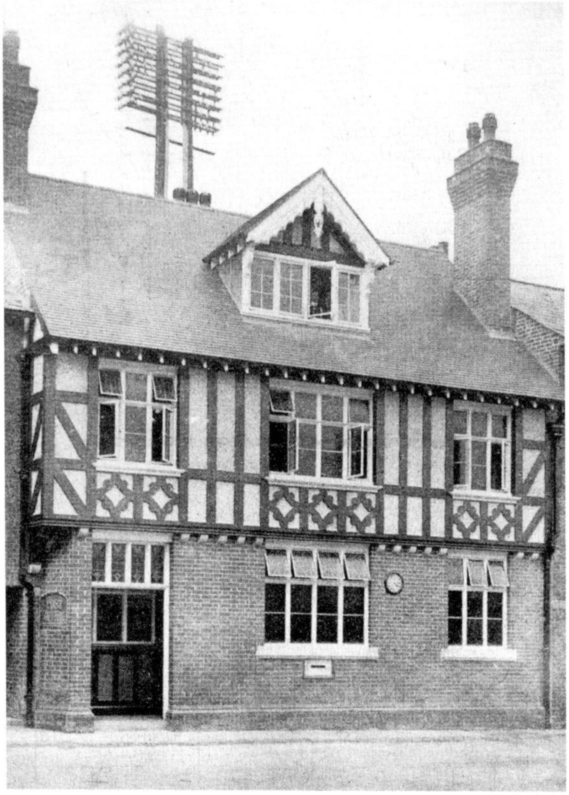

Left: *The red-brick mock-Tudor Post Office at No.3 Corn Square was built in 1908 at a cost of £2,500; this photograph was taken shortly after completion. The building's other function as the telephone exchange is evidenced by the lines emanating from the 'tree' on the roof.*

Below: *Postmen Heber Nicholas and Alfred Reece pose on their new motor cycle combinations in 1935, before setting off from the rear of Leominster Post Office on their rural rounds.*

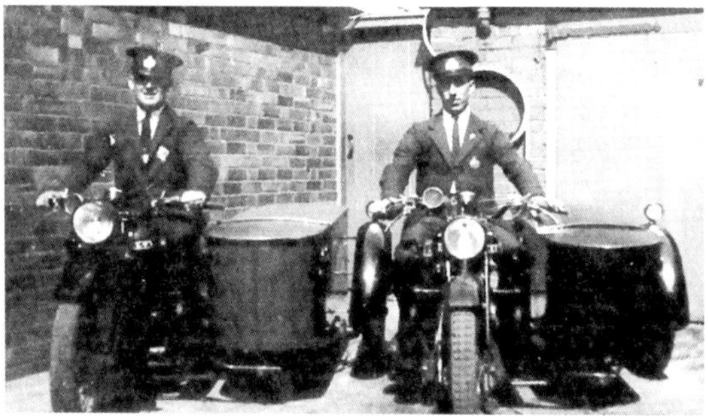

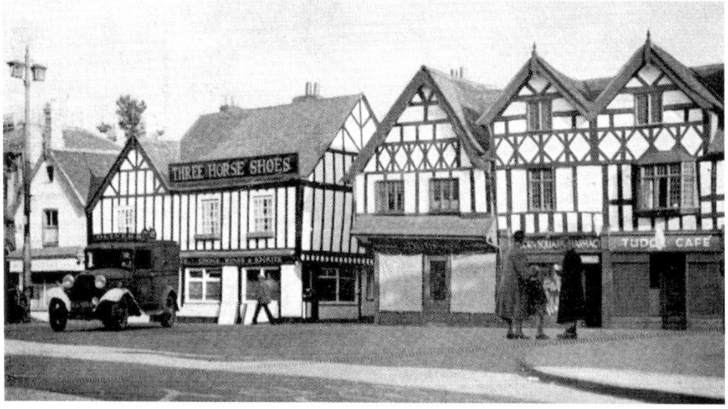

Left: *Despite its apparently good position overlooking Corn Square from the corner of School Lane, the Three Horse Shoes Inn, built around 1600, had a succession of landlords from 1922 to 1937. Could it be that the townsmen simply did not have enough spare cash during the prolonged depression of the 1920s and 30s to encourage John Hatton, James Foster, Walter Phillips and Harry James to stay for any length of time? It may have had better times for in 1891, when Tom Mitchell was landlord, he was listed as a wine and spirit merchant and mineral-water bottler. By 1902 he had moved his business to the Bird in Hand public house at No.44 Broad Street, where his widow later continued the same business, selling wines and spirits, manufacturing mineral water, and bottling ale and beer.*

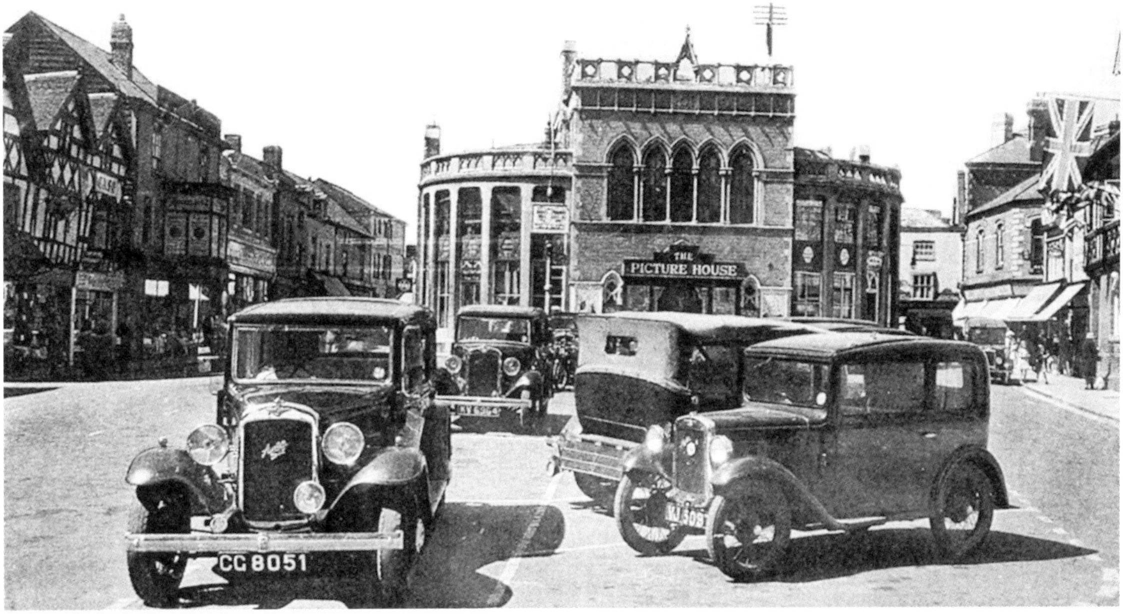

Centrally sited in a fertile valley, much of Leominster's wealth has for centuries depended on trade in agricultural produce. To keep this valuable trade away from Worcester and Hereford, the Corporation built the first Corn Exchange here in 1803 for the sale of corn and hops. On 9 June 1859 the Corn Exchange Company opened a replacement to this earlier, inconvenient building. Costing £4,000, it was designed by Birmingham architect, James Branson, and was brick-built with Bath-stone facings. It had a glass roof to give the dealers good light in which to examine the farmers' samples. The hall could seat 500 people and was used for a variety of lectures, concerts, and theatrical performances. The Corn Exchange Company, whose proprietor was J.B. Dowding, went into liquidation in 1922, when Leominster Cinema Company, who had been showing films there since 1912, took it over to screen the latest offerings of the cinema age.
Forty years later it had again outlived its usefulness and it was demolished in about 1966 to make way for shops.

SAMUEL SAMPSON,
AUCTIONEER,
Valuer, Estate, House & Insurance Agent,
4 CORN SQUARE, LEOMINSTER,
AND CATTLE MARKET, HEREFORD.
——o——
Sales of Stock in Hereford Market every Wednesday and on Fair Days at Leominster.

Left: *Samuel Sampson was a successful auctioneer in Leominster, Hereford and Ludlow from the 1860s until the end of the century.*

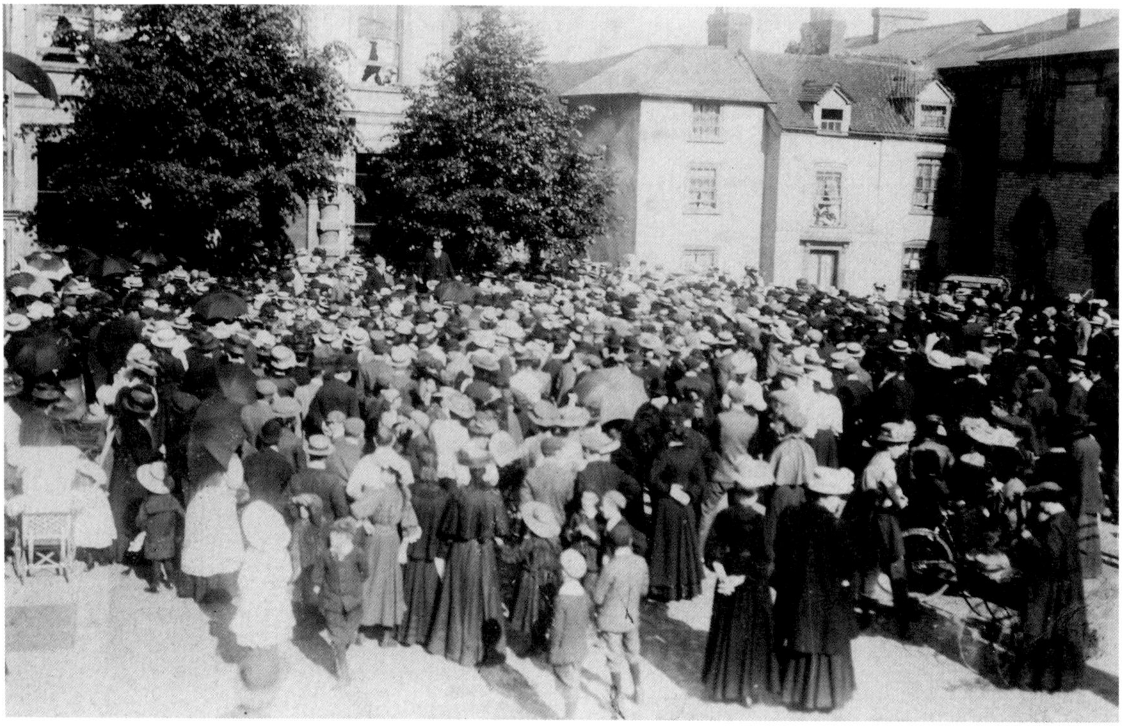

Above: *Gypsy Smith, christened Rodney, was born of Romany parents in Hertfordshire in 1860. At the age of fifteen he began his life-long evangelical work, which was to take him the length and breadth of the British Isles and twice around the world, spreading his Methodist interpretation of the word of God. He was a hugely popular speaker, attracting large crowds wherever he appeared, and he claimed to have made converts at all his meetings. King George VI was so impressed with his work that he awarded him the OBE; Gypsy Smith died in 1947. This postcard from 1908 records his visit to Leominster, where he spoke in Corn Square to a large gathering of interested townsfolk.*

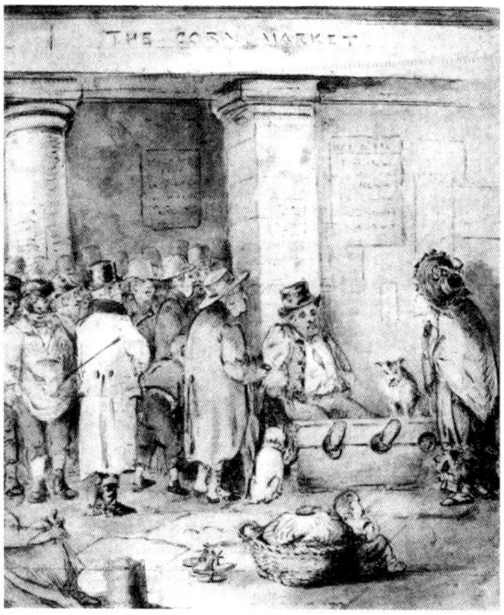

Right: *An ancient form of punishment for minor transgressors of the law was to be locked in the stocks for a number of hours. In Leominster the stocks were kept in the old Corn Exchange and only brought out on market days, when wrongdoers were exhibited to the crowd as their punishment. The Quakers, however, disapproved of public punishments as demeaning to everyone involved. In Henry Newman's 1851 depiction of a scene in front of the Corn Exchange, Leominster townsfolk seem indifferent to the man's plight, while an old Quaker is consoling the miscreant.*

Etnam Street and the Railway Station

Etnam Street, the A44, was the main road connecting Leominster to central England, leading to Bromyard and thence to Worcester. Although a main street in the town, it contained few public buildings and was very much a secondary shopping area interspersed with a variety of housing and some industries. The wide street came alive on market days as cattle and horses were sold there until a proper stock market was built. Its eastward course was deflected in 1853 by the Shrewsbury to Hereford railway, with the present road turning south towards industrial estates, before crossing the railway on a new replacement bridge.

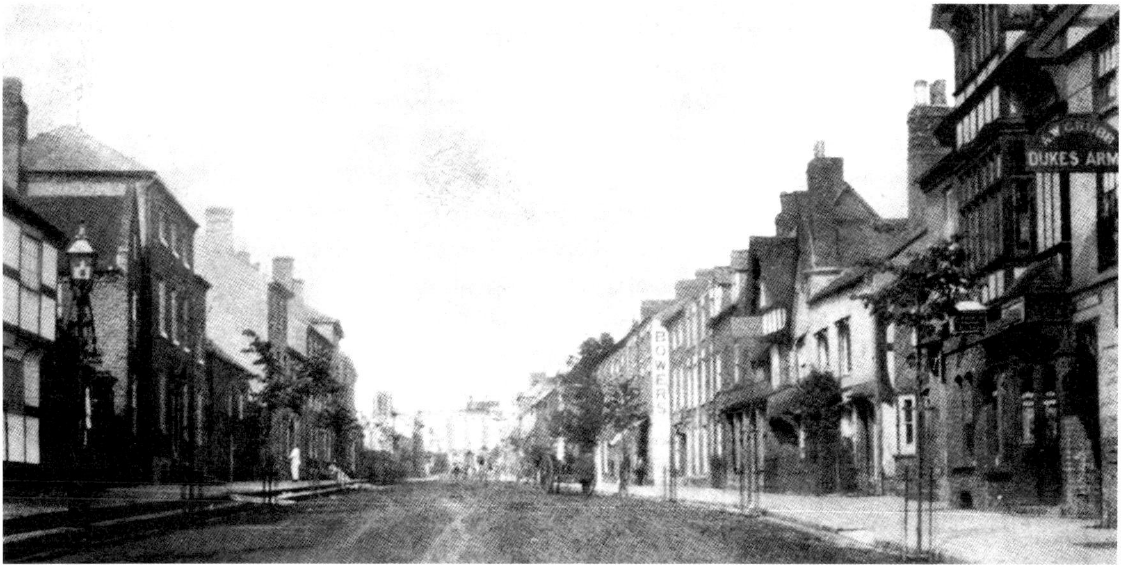

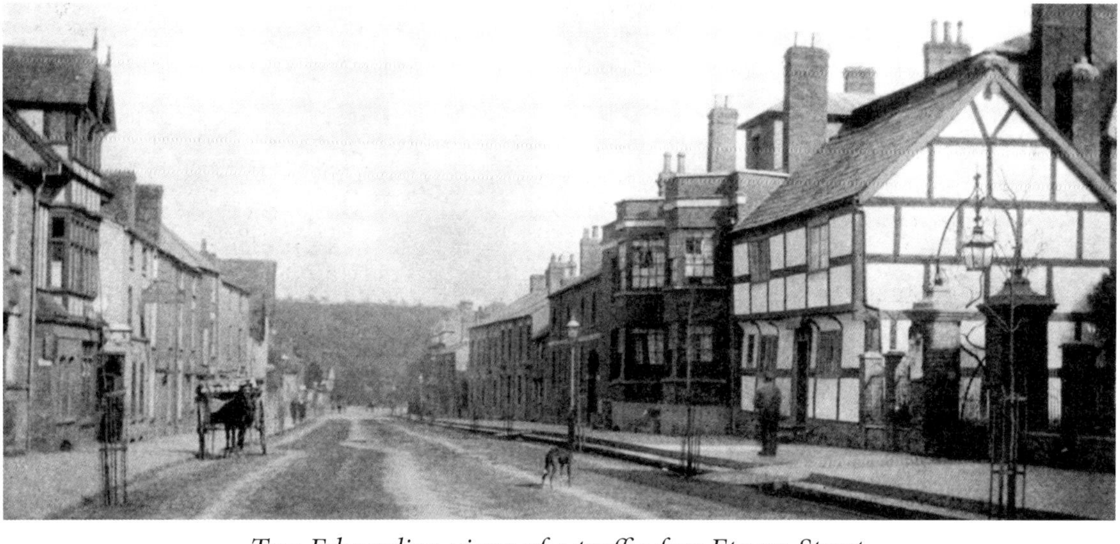

Two Edwardian views of a traffic-free Etnam Street.

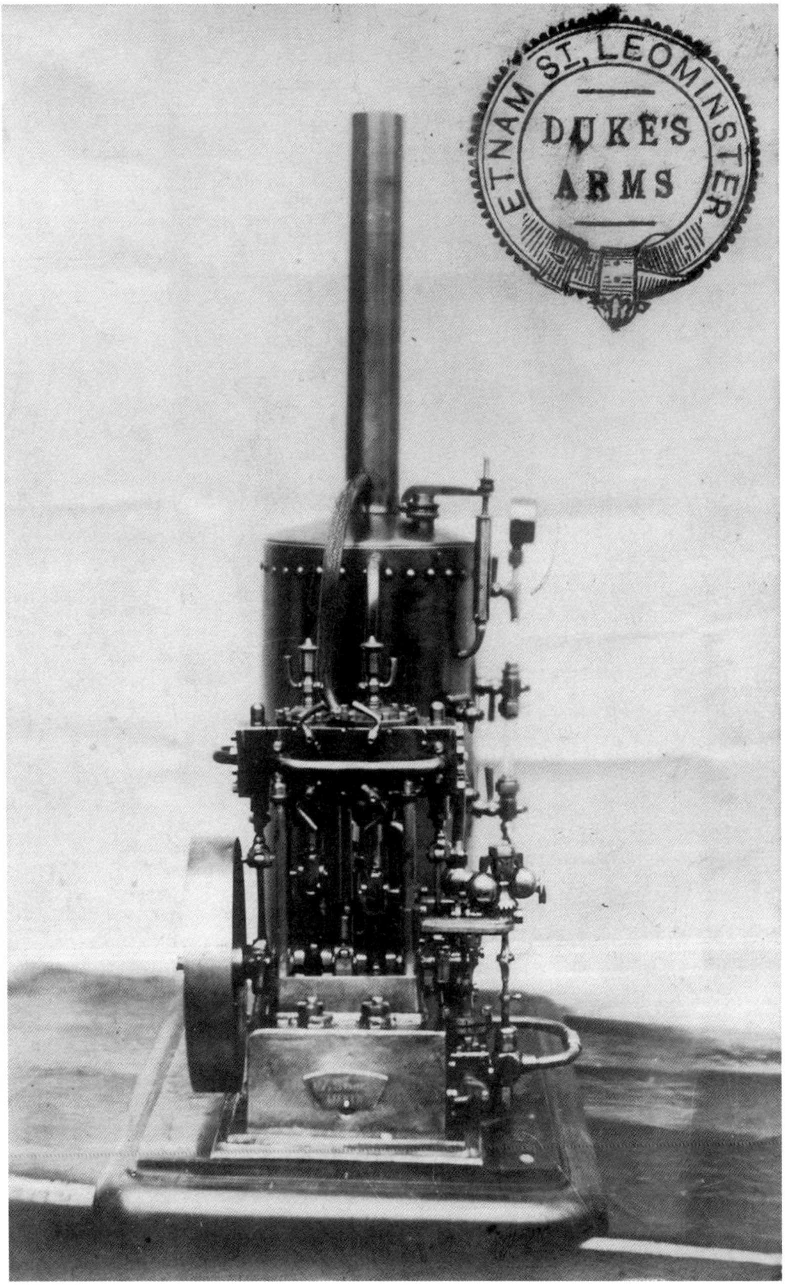

The Duke's Arms was at No.75 Etnam Street, on the right of the top photograph on the previous page. Why was this photograph of a small vertical steam engine with a nameplate inscribed 'W. Shaw Maker' made into a postcard with the Duke's Arms address? The card is of early 20th century date – in 1909 William Standage was the landlord.

Stage Waggons and Railways

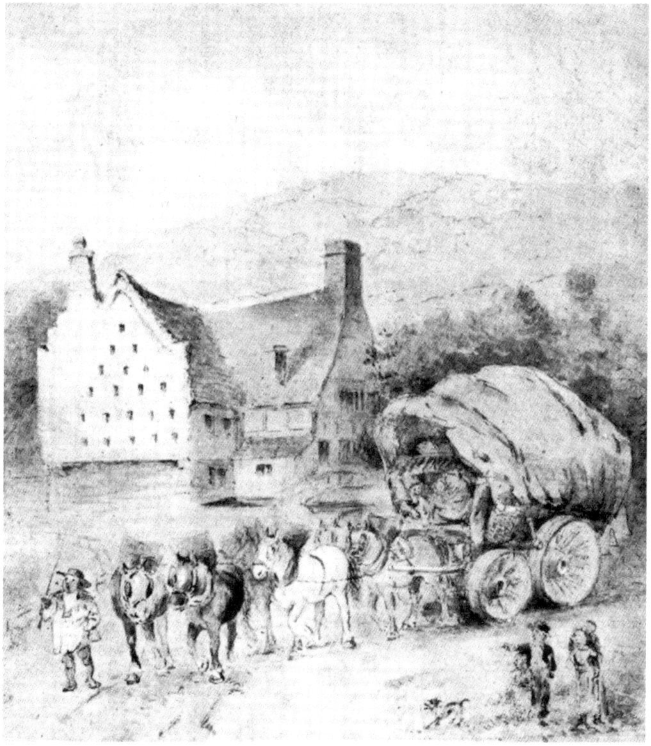

On the last mile of its journey from the direction of Worcester, a large stage waggon, drawn by a team of six horses, lumbers past the White Lion Inn, with a dovecote built into its west wall, into Etnam Street. This 1850 sketch shows the cumbersome method of transporting goods across the country to towns not on a navigable waterway, before the arrival of the railway. Massively built waggons could carry heavy loads of up to eight tons and ran on wheels with rims nine inches wide with sixteen-inch hubs. Wheels of this size were needed to cope with the severe jolting caused by uneven road surfaces. These were reduced to a quagmire in wet weather when the fragile, badly-maintained surface frequently broke up. The waggoner had to walk beside the lead horse for he could be heavily fined for riding on the horse or the waggon. Freight charges varied between 1s. 6d. to 2s. per hundredweight. Travellers who could not afford the stage coach fares sometimes travelled under the canvas cover amongst the bales of freight. Like the stage-coach routes, a similar web of waggon routes covered the country, with staging posts to change the horses.

Some idea of the extensive network and the time the waggons spent travelling from London can be gleaned from this extract taken from an advertisement in the *Hereford Journal* of 18 January, 1809:

> The proprietors of the Cambrian Waggon Company beg leave most respectfully to inform the public that they have established a regular conveyance to and from London, Oxford, Cheltenham, Glocester [*sic*], Worcester, Manchester, Liverpool, Leeds, Halifax, Saddleworth, Huddersfield, Wakefield, Sheffield, Birmingham, Ludlow, Chester, Shrewsbury and all parts of the North of England and Scotland. For Herefordshire, Monmouthshire and all parts of South Wales and the South of Ireland, their London waggons set out from the Cambrian Warehouse, Bell Inn, Smithfield, London every Saturday morning and will call going out and coming in at the Dolphin, Oxford Street, Pack Horse Inn, Worcester Tuesday night, Cambrian Warehouse Bromyard Wednesday morning, Hereford Thursday morning, Hay Thursday night, Brecon Sunday evening, Llandovery Monday morning … and arrive at

Carmarthen Tuesday Noon, from where all goods for Cardiganshire, Pembrokeshire and the South of Ireland will be regularly forwarded. All goods intended for this conveyance from Manchester, Birmingham etc. are particularly requested to be directed and forwarded by Twiss from Manchester and Stockall from Birmingham to the Pack Horse at Worcester and also from Glocester [*sic*] and the clothing country, by Page to the Cambrian Warehouse Hereford. … Their Bristol waggons return from the Cambrian Warehouse Brecon Saturday evening, Abergavenny Saturday night and arrive at the Moderator Warehouse Newport on Monday Morning, when all goods for Bristol, Bath and the West of England will be regularly forwarded by the Moderator boat to Bristol and from there by different carriers.

In 1801 North's Cambrian Waggon Company called at the Talbot Hotel in Leominster, but by 1808 they had a warehouse in Corn Square from where a network of other carriers radiated. Horse-drawn transport persisted until it was replaced by motorized delivery vans. As late as 1902, on market days a network of 39 carriers based at pubs in Leominster carried supplies to the surrounding villages, despite the penetration of the county by the railway.

Until the arrival of the railway, stage-coaches carried passengers around the county. In 1808, Broome, Whitney and Co. operated a twice-weekly service from Hereford through Leominster to Shrewsbury on Tuesdays and Fridays, taking all day for the journey. Travelling inside, the fare from Hereford to Shrewsbury was £1 2s., and outside was 12s. From Hereford to Leominster the fare was 5s. inside and 3s. outside; parcels were carried at 1½d. per pound. The journey time from Hereford to Shrewsbury was reduced to an hour and a half by train instead of a whole day by stage-coach.

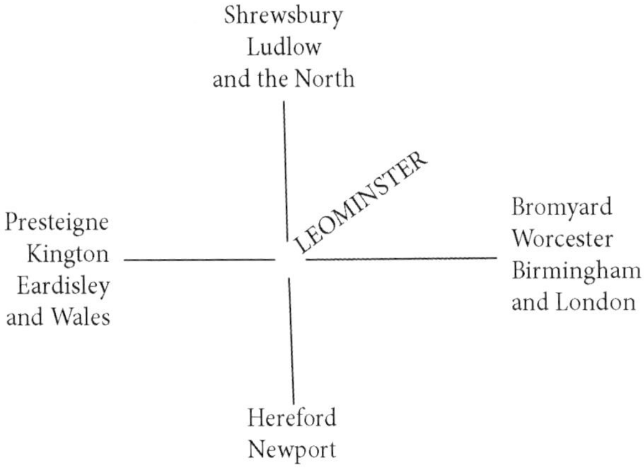

The railway between Shrewsbury and Hereford was opened on 6 December 1853 with great rejoicings, and branch lines westwards from Leominster to Kington and Presteigne, and eastwards to Tenbury and Bromyard were in the planning stages. At long last goods and produce could flow rapidly and cheaply in and out of Herefordshire. The line to Kington via Titley was opened in August 1857, with a later branch line from Titley to Eardisley in 1874 where it joined the Hereford, Hay and Brecon line. A year later a branch line to Presteigne and an extension from Kington to New Radnor were opened. The final stage of the Worcester, Bromyard, Leominster line was opened in September 1897 – the last railway line laid in the county, connecting directly to the Midlands.

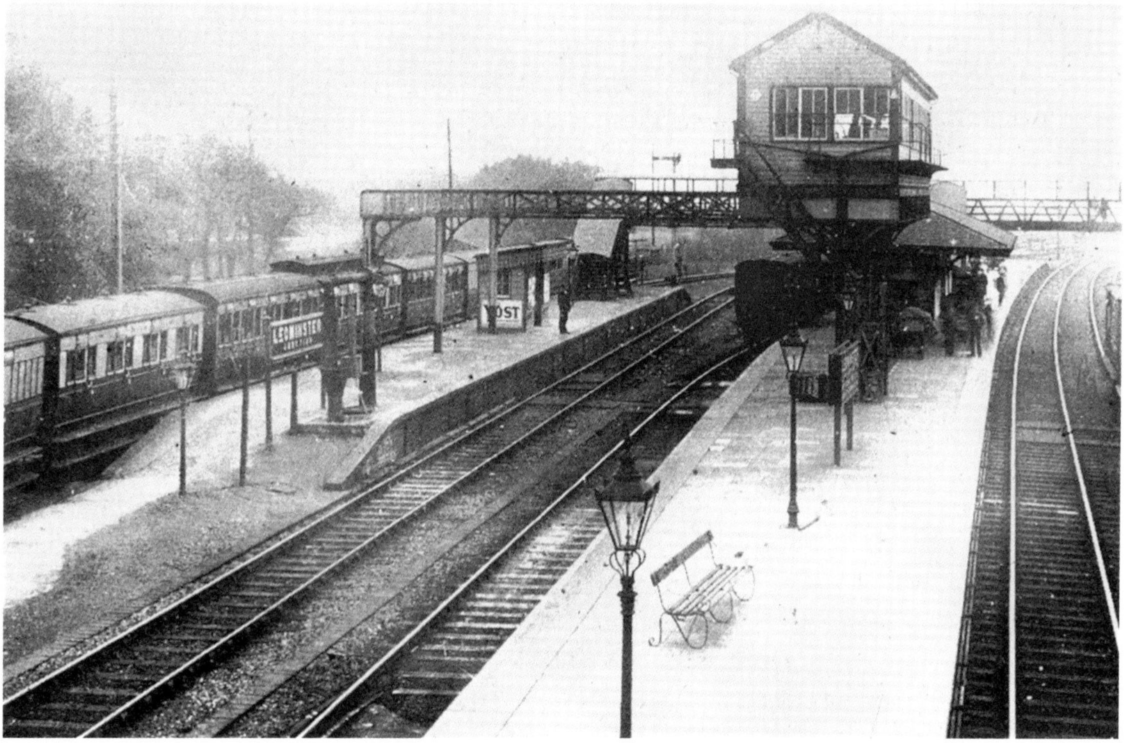

Above: *The name board on this 1908 postcard reads 'Leominster Junction', revealing the town's importance to the rural villages. The dominating feature of the station was the centrally placed signal box, built in 1901 and finally dismantled in 1958.*

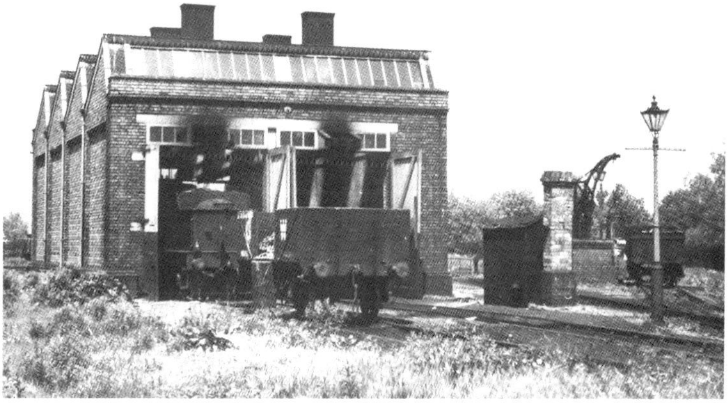

Right: *Steam locomotives, used for local work, were regularly cleaned and maintained in the Leominster engine shed. This photograph from about 1960 shows the shed just before steam engines were phased out. Like many workshops built before the advent of electric lighting, the building incorporated extensive factory-style roof-lights; the chimney-like structures were designed to act as smoke-vents, but for the men, the working atmosphere was very dirty. For major overhauls or repairs, locomotives would be taken to the engine works at Swindon or Wolverhampton.*

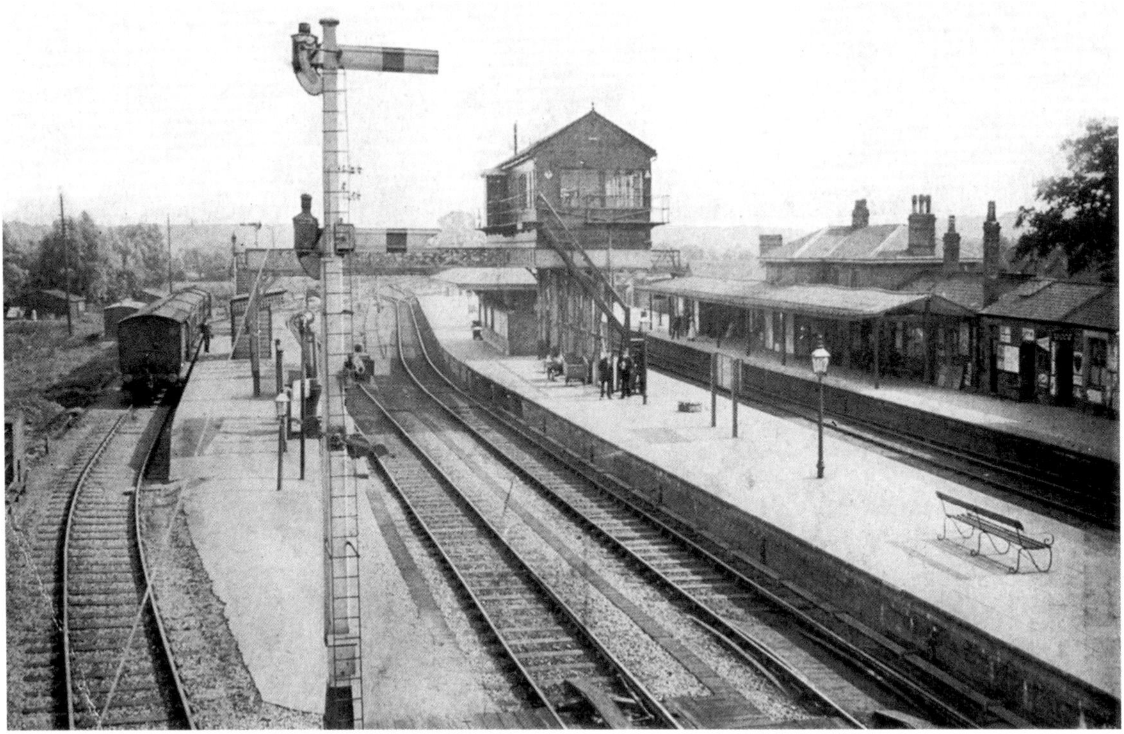

Above: *This overall view of Leominster station shows the five platforms in use during its most prosperous period in 1910. The train for Worcester stands at the platform on the left.*

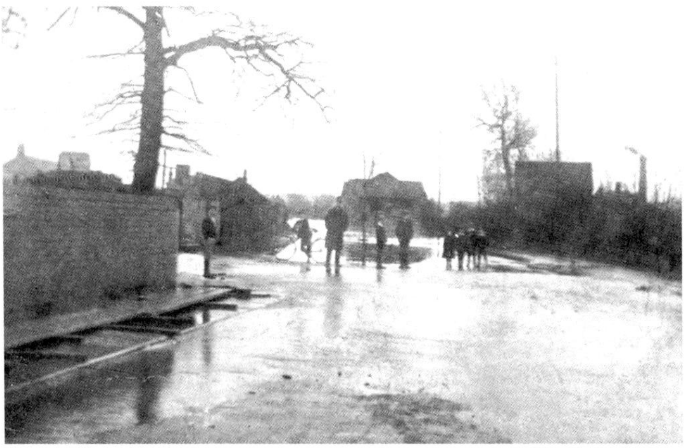

Right: *The confluence of the Pinsley Brook and the River Lugg frequently flooded the Worcester Road near to the approach to the railway station. The December 1910 floods were particularly deep and long-lasting, so that a raised board-walk was placed along the pavement to keep passengers' feet dry. Warehouses and factories now line the road, but the tree and the brick building in the centre are a reminder of its previous appearance. The smoking chimney on the right was part of the water pumping station.*

Right: *This 1970s view looks north towards the abandoned goods yard and the station beyond the bend. Just south of the old iron bridge that carried the A44 Worcester road over the tracks stood Leominster South signal box. The photograph clearly shows the layout of the tracks and sidings at that time.*

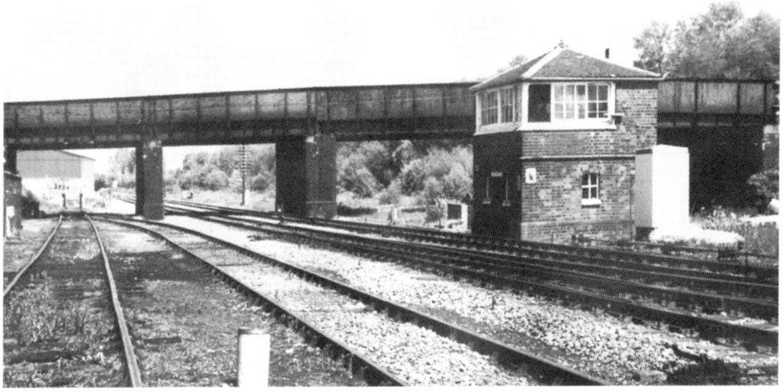

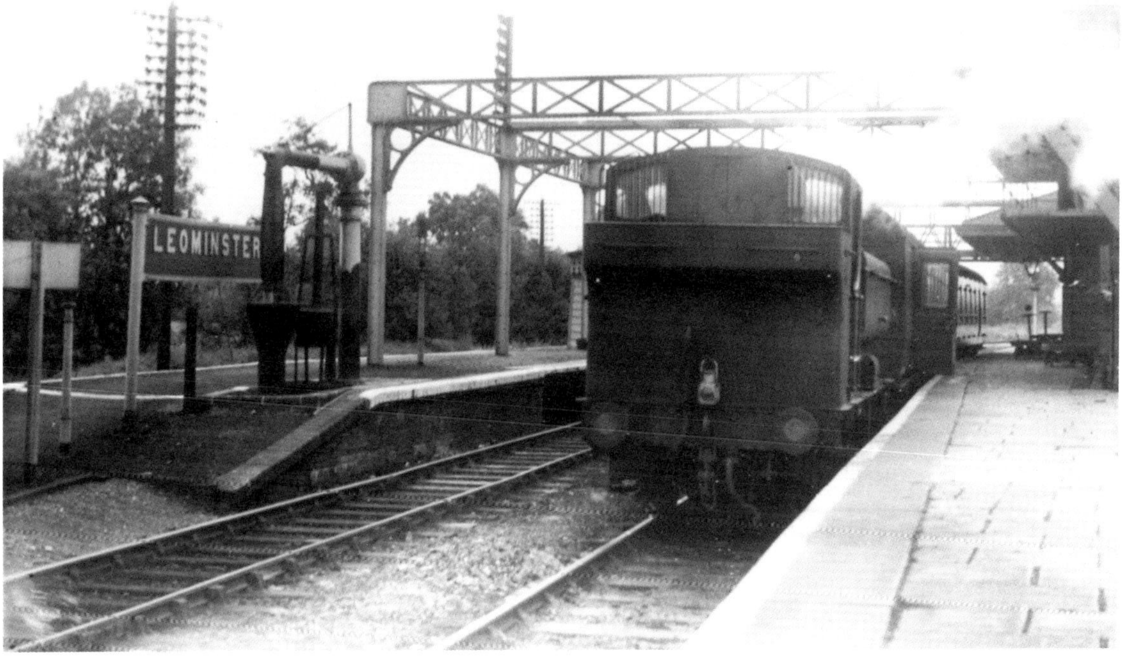

Above: *Leominster station about 1960 during the last days of steam power.*

The convenience of car, lorry and bus transport eventually reduced the importance of these minor railway lines. They served scattered communities but generated little profit and could not remain open without large subsidies. When the inevitable closures occurred, many people regretted their passing, saying that cheaper ways of operating them should have been explored before their final closure in the 1960s. Realistically, however, it was a case of 'Use it or lose it'. Leominster is one of only four railway stations remaining open in the county where once, in the railways' heyday, there were nearly fifty stations and halts serving the community.

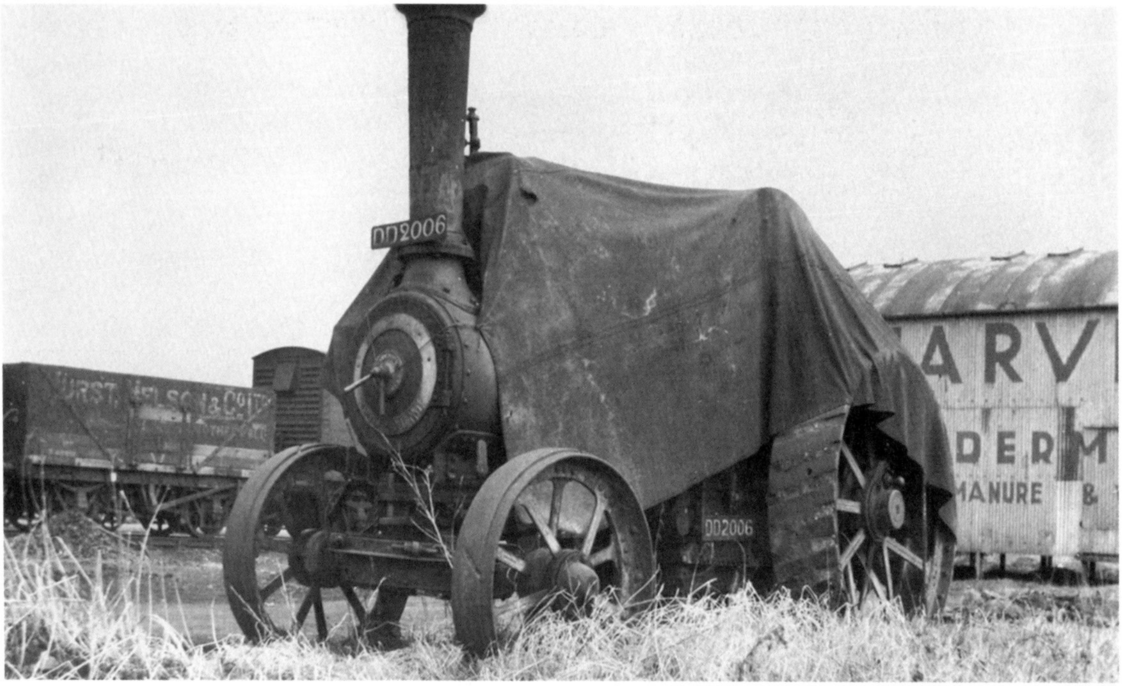

A redundant Alchin compound steam engine registration number DD 2006, stands abandoned under a tarpaulin cover in Leominster goods yard in the 1950s. For decades these traction engines moved heavy loads from railway stations to destinations around the country. In the background of the photograph, J.P. Harvey's corrugated iron shed was used to store artificial fertilizer destined for delivery to local farms.

CARRIERS TO—

Aymestrey.—Frederick Bywaters, from the *Talbot Inn*, Fridays.
Bromyard.—Henry Franklin, from his house, West Street, Mondays.
Dilwyn.—Edward Edwards, from the *Ring of Bells Inn*, Fridays.
Eardisland.—William Williams, from the *Talbot Inn*, Tuesdays and Fridays; Samuel Prosser, from *Radnorshire Arms*, Tuesdays.
Kingsland.—Jane Mason, from *White Hart Inn*, Fridays.
Kington.—Samuel Prosser, from *Radnorshire Arms*, Tuesdays, at 6 a.m., returning the same days.
Pembridge.—William Williams, from the *Talbot Inn*, Tuesdays and Fridays; Samuel Prosser, from *Radnorshire Arms*, Tuesdays.
Presteigne.—Samuel Prosser, from *Radnorshire Arms*, occasionally.
Pudleston.—Thomas Adams, from *White Swan*, about 4 p.m. Fridays.
Shobdon.—J. Griffiths, from *Elephant and Castle*, Tuesdays and Fridays.
Weobley.—Payne, from *Ring of Bells Inn*, Fridays.
Wigmore.—Frederick Bywaters, from *Talbot Inn*, Fridays.
Worcester.—Samuel Prosser, from *Radnorshire Arms*, Thursdays, returning on Saturdays; Henry Franklin, from his house, West Street, Mondays.

Leominster carriers from the 1867 Littlebury's Directory.

Burgess Street, Bargates and West Street

Burgess Street

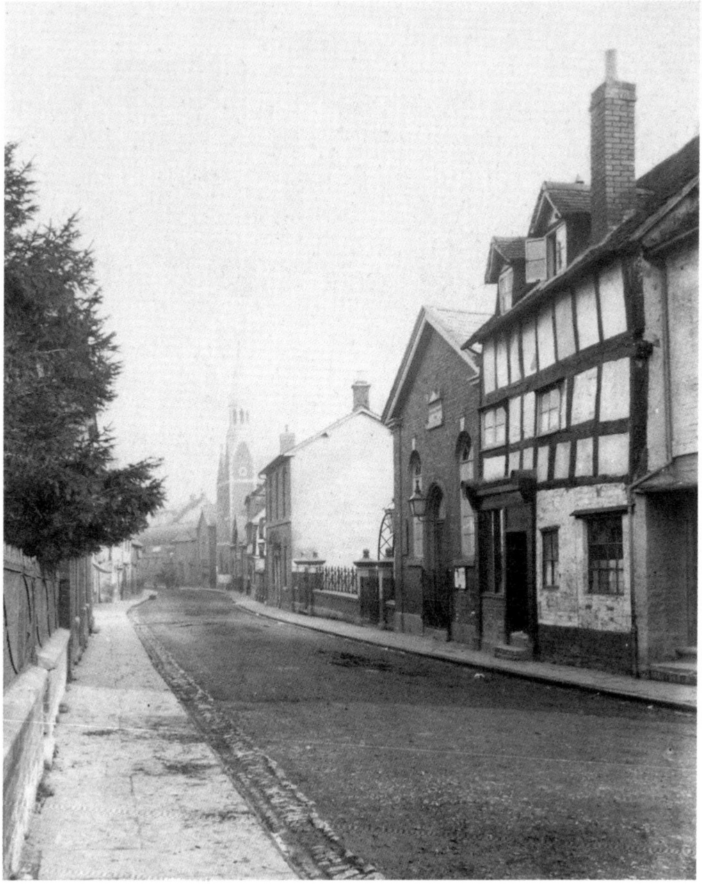

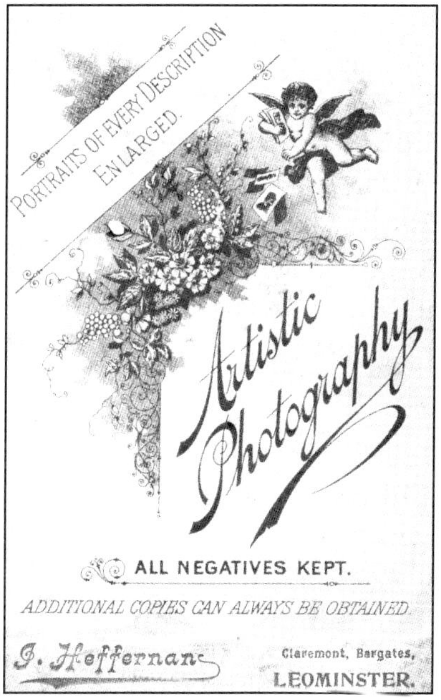

It was around 1900 when J. Heffernan photographed the south side of Burgess Street from its junction with Rainbow Street. In the middle distance and near the centre of the photograph, the 80 foot high tower of the Congregational church was a landmark to rival the Town Hall clock tower. Built in 1867 by James Page of Leominster at a cost of £1,600, the church's 250 seats were crowded for its opening on 4 June 1867. The white-washed Mission Hall, or Meeting House, was built in 1840 and has had a variety of occupants, said to include the Roman Catholics as well as the Church of Christ, the Y.M.C.A., and a Mission Room with an adult school. It is now a ladies' hairdressers. Beyond this was the Magistrates Court and the police station staffed by a superintendent, two sergeants and sixteen constables, several of whom lived in now demolished houses along the street. Solicitors' offices now occupy the half-timbered house on the corner.

Burgess Street

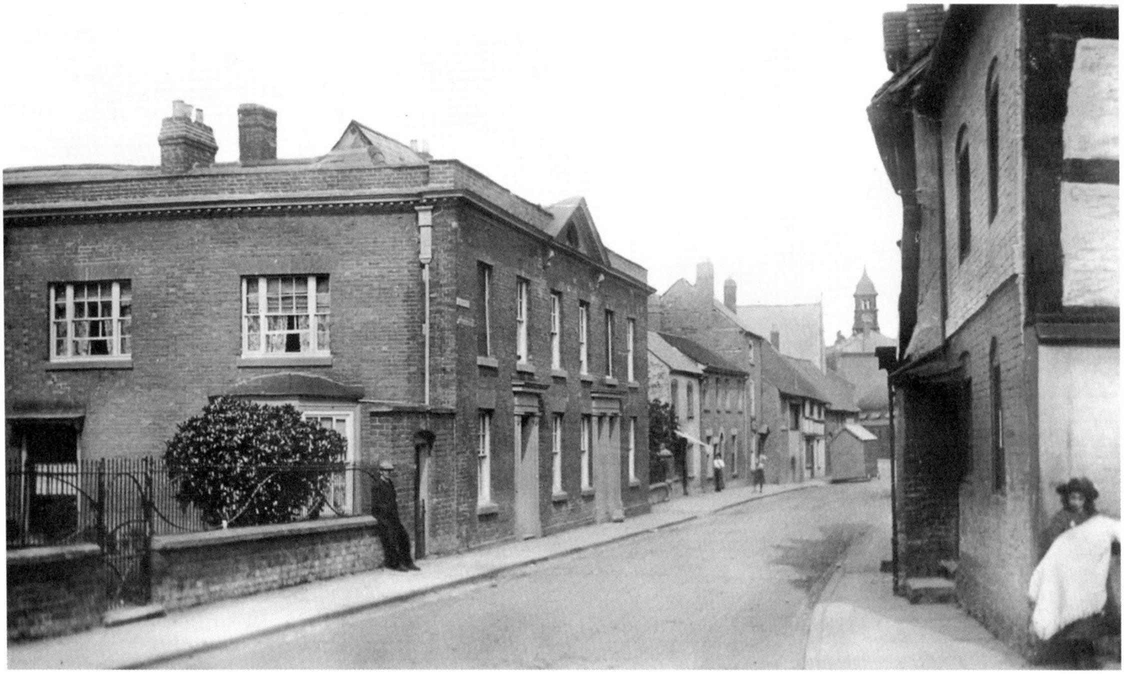

Above: *A 1910 view of the north side of Burgess Street seen from its junction with Rainbow Street. In 1885 Grafton House, seen on the left, became the meeting place of Sidney Black's religious group, 'The Church of Christ'. They later moved to the Mission Hall on the other side of the street. To the left of the distant Town Hall clock tower, the roof of the Wesleyan Chapel is just visible.*

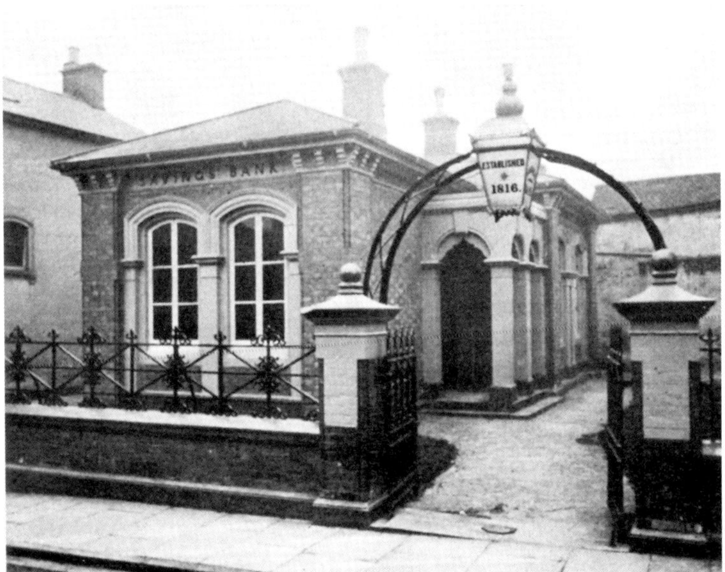

Above: *Leominster Savings Bank was first established in 1816. These solid brick premises in Burgess Street were built in 1857 at a cost of £700, demonstrating its prosperity.*

Bargates

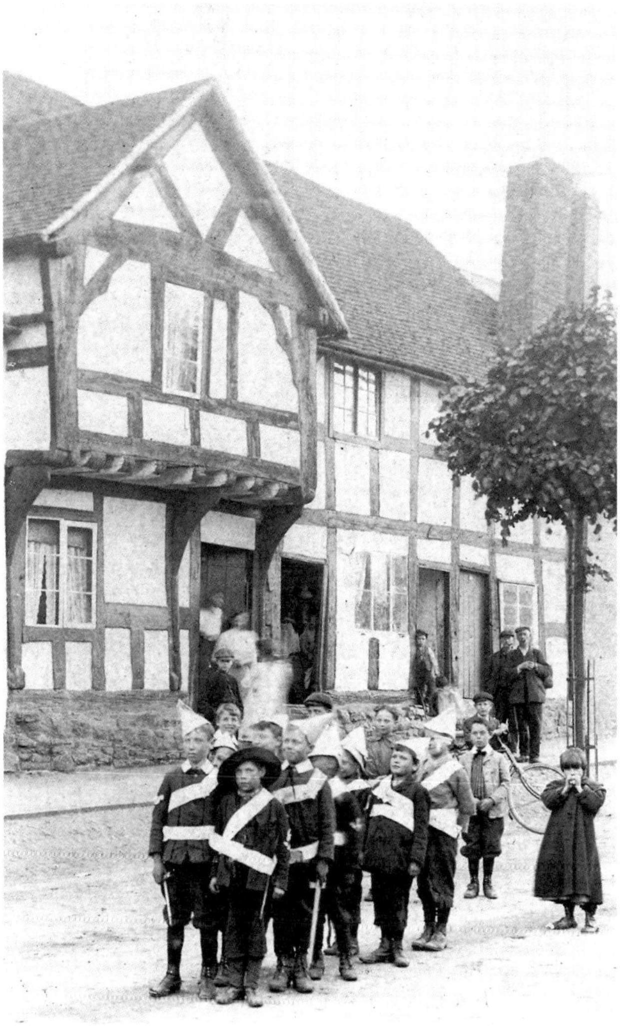

Left: *In 1908 Britain's defences were being reformed as the military and naval arms race with Germany gathered pace. Dressed up as soldiers, these ten lads parade in the traffic-free street, watched by amused relatives and neighbours. Like all little boys, they copied the actions of their elder brothers, fathers and friends, who had joined the reorganised 1st Battalion of the Herefordshire Regiment in Leominster's 'F' Company. The photographer, perhaps unknowingly, reveals the innocence of the boys' military fervour and patriotism. Only a few years later, as young soldiers, they would experience the horrors of a war quite unimaginable in their boyhood games.*

This delightful photograph shows a traffic-free Lower Bargates, opposite Bengry's petrol pumps and very close to the site of the present traffic lights. After a bitter controversy this picturesque row of cottages was demolished in the 1960s to create a short-lived entrance to the new bus and car park. A small flower-bed, bollards and a pedestrian way now mark this lost treasure.

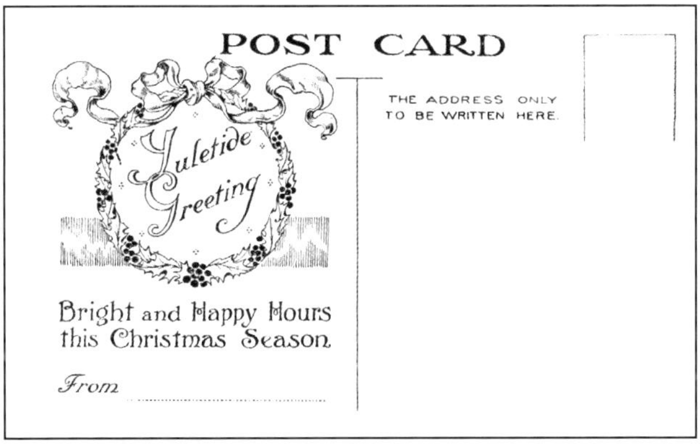

Left: *On the address side of the above photograph is a Christmas card design.*

West Street

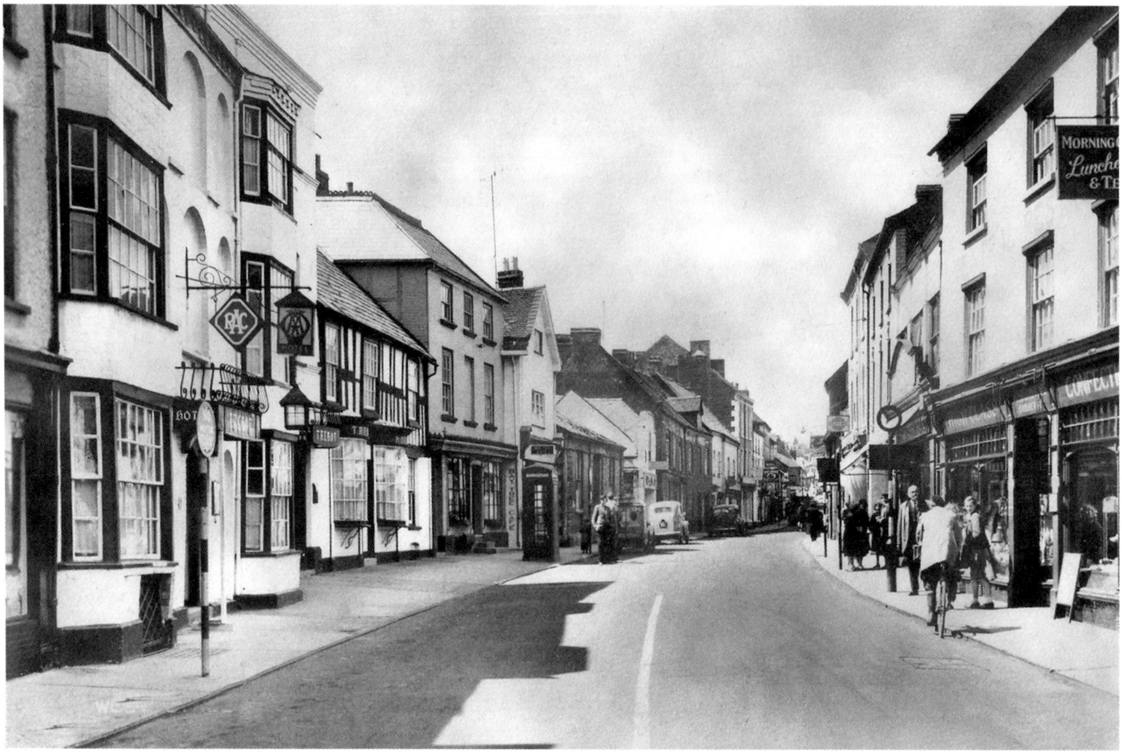

Before the cattle market was built in the 19th century, cows and beef cattle were sold in West and Dishley Streets. Little, except the shop owners, appears to have changed since this 1950s photograph of West Street was taken. The Talbot Hotel is on the left.

W. M. BRIMFIELD,
BUILDER, CONTRACTOR,
Timber Dealer, Slate & Tile Merchant,
38 WEST STREET, LEOMINSTER.

Dealer in all kinds of Building Materials, including Door Sashes and Frames, Mouldings and Skirting, Broseley Tiles, Slate Flooring Tiles, Glazed Socket Pipes, Plain and Fancy Ridges, and all kinds of Fire-Clay Goods on hand.

RELIABLE
Boots & Shoes
BEST POSSIBLE VALUE.
J. H. THORNE,
12 West St., Leominster.

West Street advertisements from two different periods.
Left: *W.M. Brimfield about 1900.*
Right: *J.H. Thorne in 1921.*

Talbot Hotel

Leominster

Herefordshire

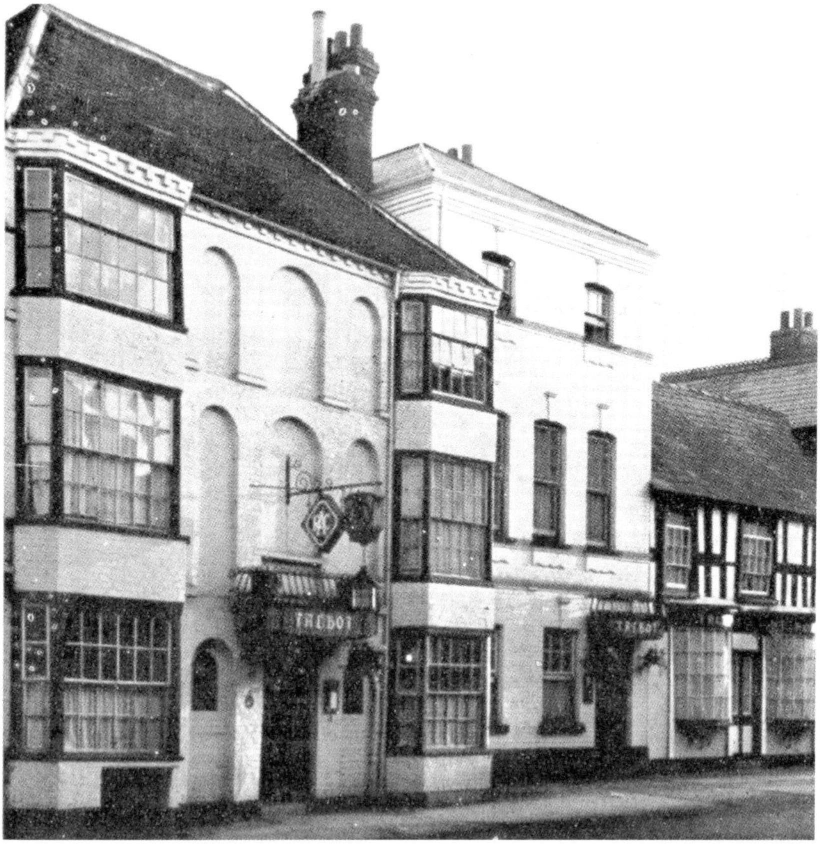

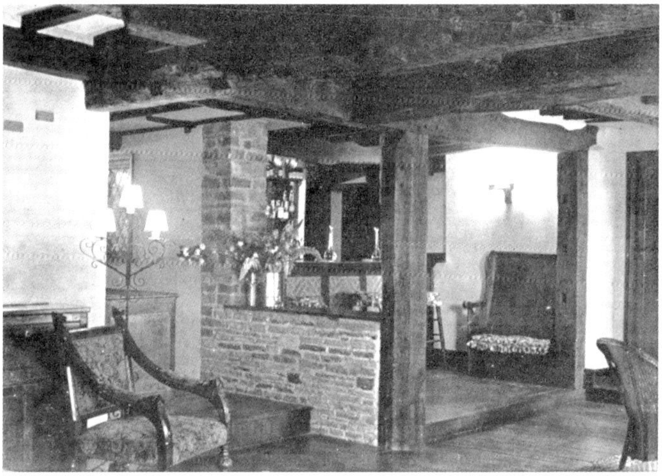

Two photographs from a 1950s advertising card for the Talbot Hotel when bed and breakfast only cost £1 7s. 6d.

Like several other large buildings in the town built before 1851, the Talbot Hotel's six bricked-in windows are reminders of people's opposition to the Window Tax. This was first introduced in England in 1696 under William III and later extended to fund the wars with France. Rates were revised in 1802 so that houses with six windows paid 8s., houses with ten windows paid £2 10s. and houses with 100 windows were rated at £52 9s. This tax was impossible to avoid, and rather than pay it many householders bricked up as many windows as was feasible. Some were re-opened after the tax was removed in 1851, but others remain bricked up to this day.

Transport Problems at the Iron Cross in 1904

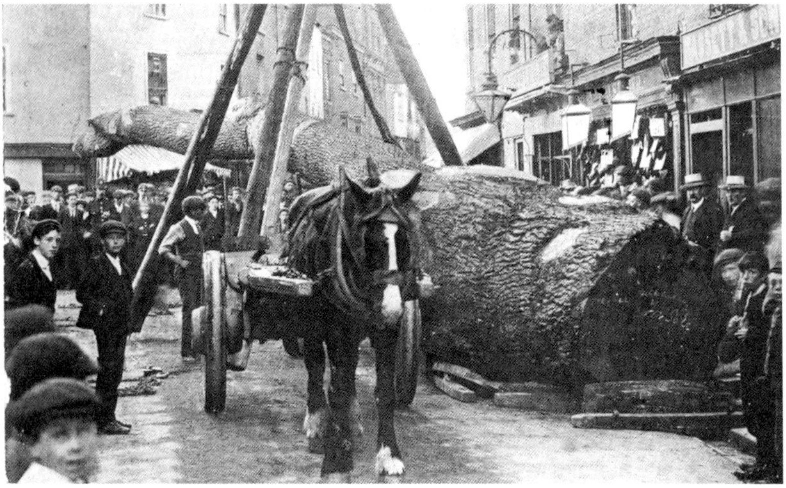

Problems occurred at the Iron Cross in August 1904 when an attempt was made to move the massive trunk of an oak tree from Burton Court, Eardisland, where it had shaded the lawn for many years, to Leominster railway station. The trunk twice fell off its carriage in attempting to negotiate the corner when a wheel appears to have collapsed under the weight and strain. How through-traffic managed to avoid the obstruction is not recorded. A report of the recovery of the oak tree that blocked the junction for two days was printed on 19 August in the Leominster News:

> At the close of the Market last Friday in the presence of a large crowd of spectators a powerful tripod was erected and after two or three hours hard labour the tree was again put on the carriage. A cheer was raised as the carriage started for the railway station. There is a large demand for postcards of the accident.

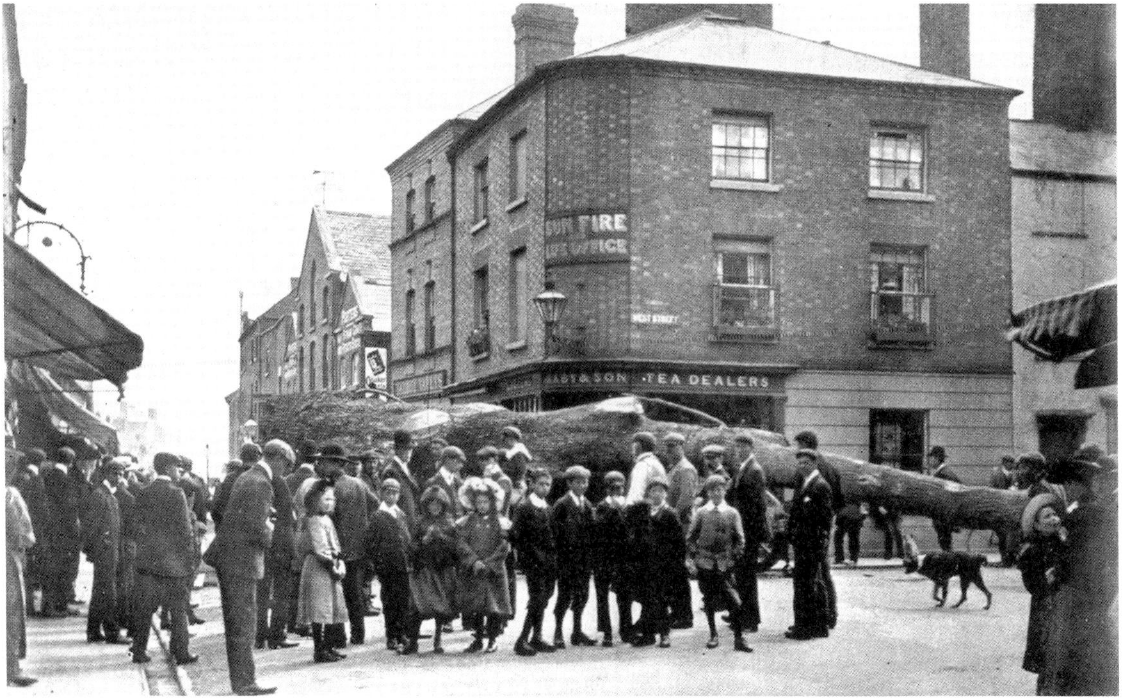

South Street

South Street continues the line of the original A49 south through the centre of the town, with West Street joining it at the Iron Cross and Etnam Street a little further on.

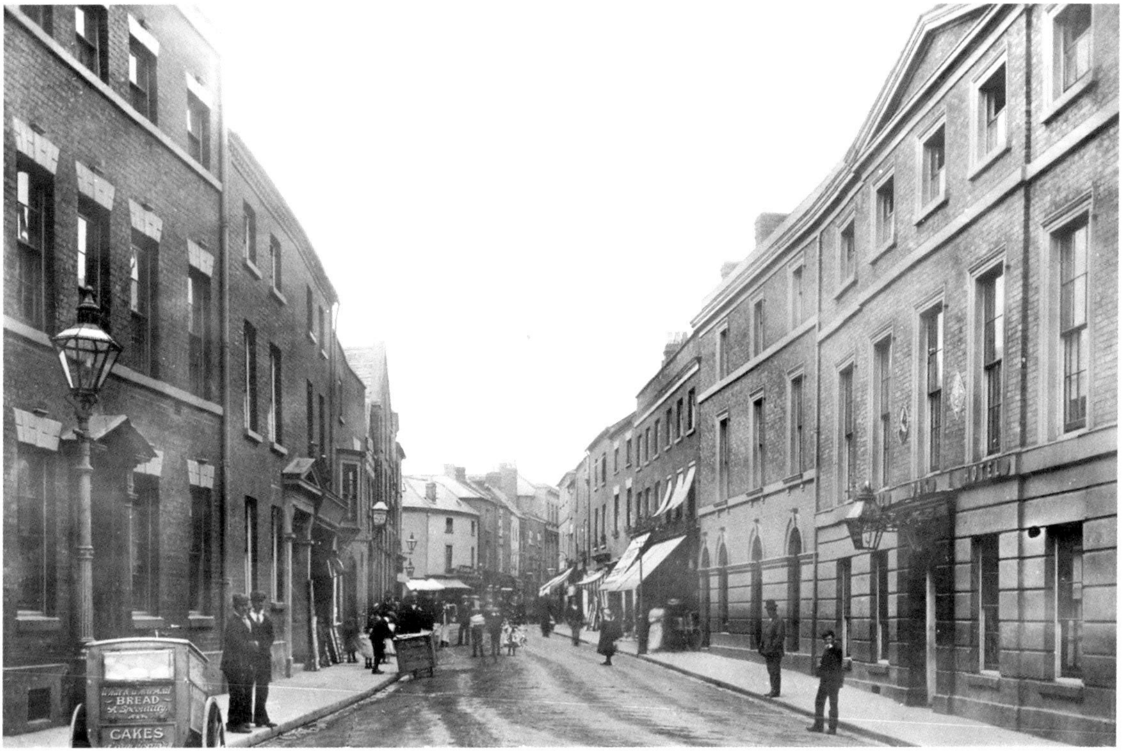

A hand-drawn baker's cart stands on the left of a traffic-free South Street looking towards the junction with West Street.
The short message on this 1910 postcard reads:

'We arrived here at No.12, lunched at the Royal Oak Hotel. Did us well. Went for a walk in the town – Market Day, some quaint streets but not much of a town'

revealing how much they must have missed.

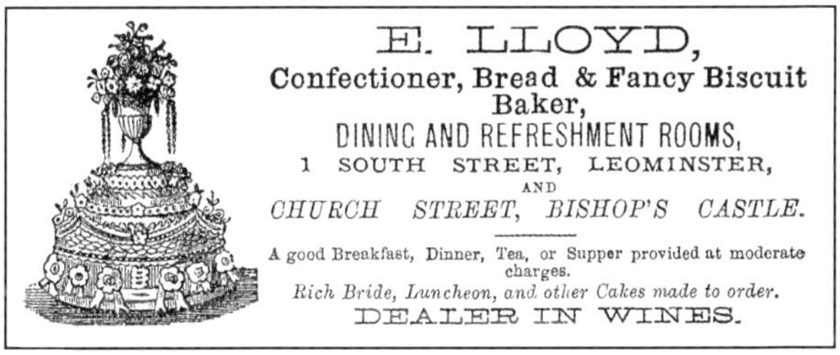

Left: *Lloyd's Dining and Refreshment Rooms at No.1 South Street, would have been close to West Street.*

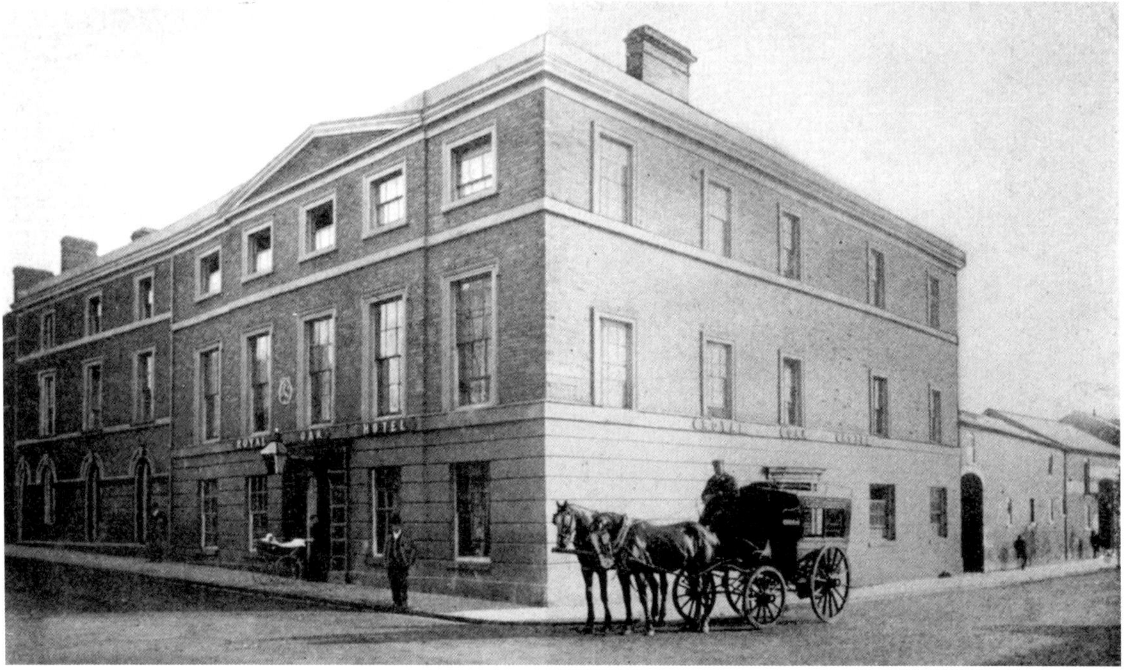

Above: *The Royal Oak Hotel is on the corner of South Street and Etnam Street and almost opposite the Talbot. Well before the internal combustion engine arrived its horse bus was advertised to meet all trains.*

Right: *The Royal Edward Order of Freemasons, Lodge No.892, held its meetings in the Royal Oak Hotel in South Street and in 1902 William Powell was Worshipful Master and John Daggs was Secretary.*

In 1918 George Butters became Worshipful Master and his installation as Provincial Grand Steward on 10 January was celebrated with a sumptuous meal. This consisted of devilled whitebait as starter, followed by roast beef and pheasant, and finished with apple tart, wine jelly, damsons and lemon sponge – this was as much as wartime shortages would allow.

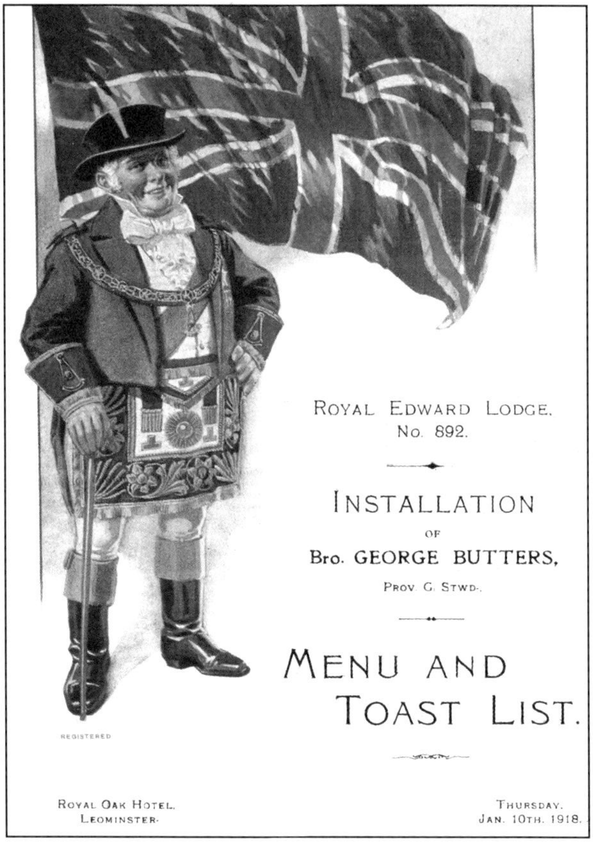

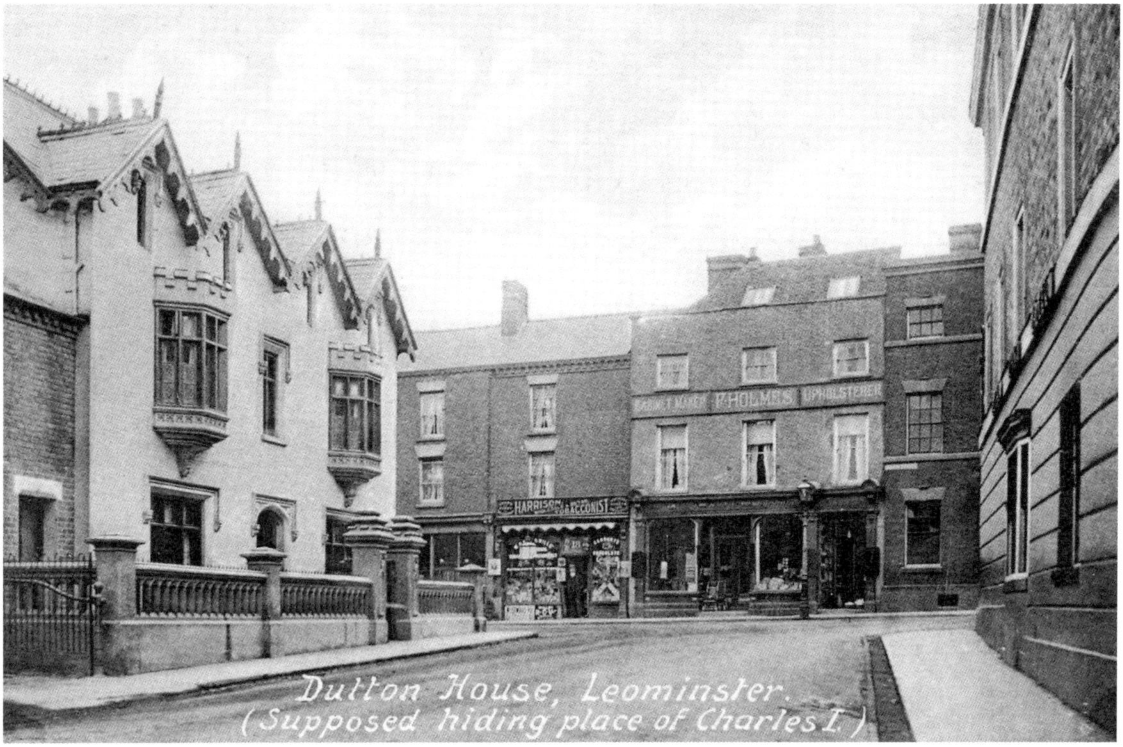

This photograph was taken from Etnam Street looking westwards towards South Street. The side wall of the Royal Oak is just visible on the right. Dutton House, built in the 16th century, but encased in a Victorian shell, is prominent on the left. In 1922 John Harrison was a tobacconist and newsagent in South Street (where he also published this postcard). Next door, for some 20 years Frederick Holmes was a furniture-maker and upholsterer in William Neal's old premises (below).
This 1920s postcard was used during the paper shortage of the Second World War.

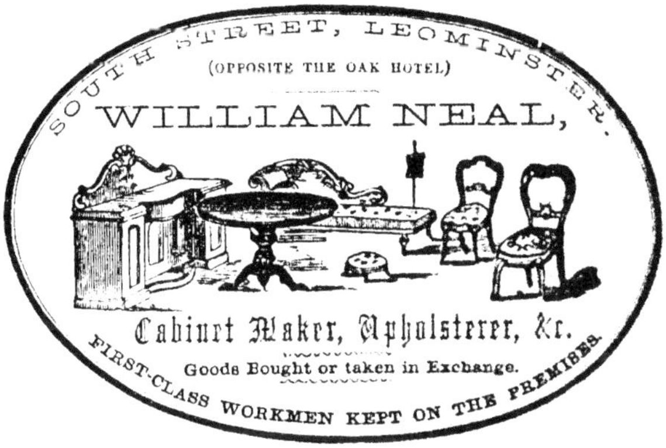

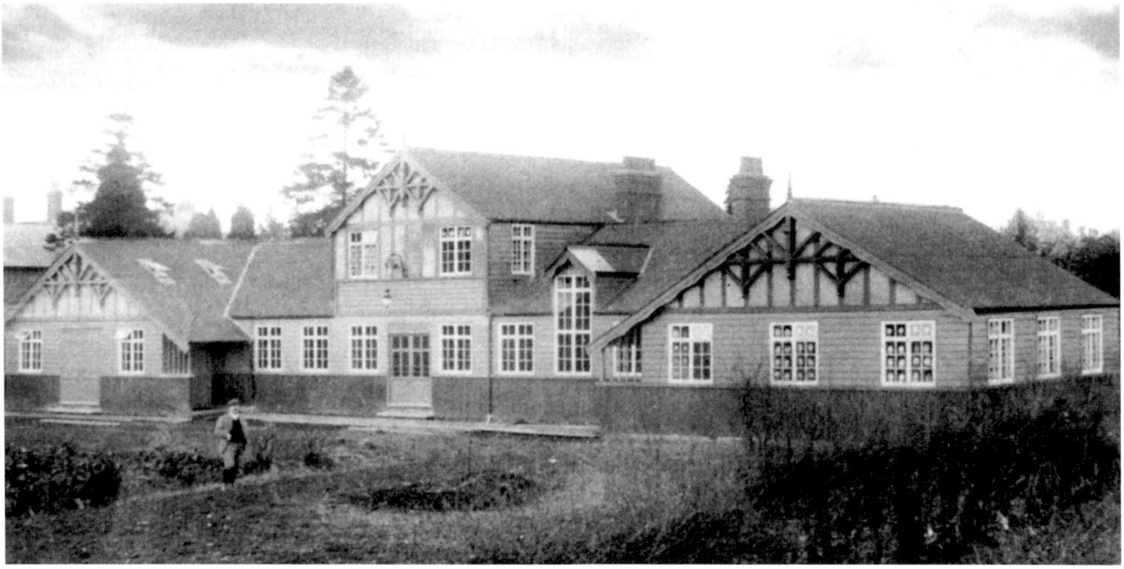

Above: *In 1906 the Church Institute was built in South Street on land behind the Friends Meeting House with an open space in front. It was an iron-framed building clad in brick, cost £1,780 and contained reading rooms, billiard rooms and a lecture hall. The building served as a parish hall until the late 1960s when it was demolished to be replaced by the new British Legion Headquarters.*

PUBLIC LIBRARY
10, SOUTH STREET, LEOMINSTER.
HARRIET WENT,
PRINTER, BOOKSELLER, STATIONER, AND
EMIGRATION AGENT.
Depôt of the Society for Promoting Christian Knowledge & of the National Society.

Left: *In the 1860s and 70s Mrs Harriet Went ran a bookshop, printers and lending library opposite the Royal Oak Hotel. In the 1870s she found a lucrative sideline as an emigration agent, organising travel arrangements for the large numbers of local people wishing to escape grinding poverty and unemployment inflicted on rural areas like Herefordshire by a severe and prolonged agricultural depression.*

PHOTOGRAPHIC ESTABLISHMENT,
36 SOUTH STREET, LEOMINSTER.
E. J. EVANS
Begs to inform the Public that his Studio is fitted up on the most scientific principles, for the production of
FIRST-CLASS PORTRAITS.
Every Picture Guaranteed, and unless highly approved another sitting given.
PARTIES WAITED UPON AT THEIR OWN RESIDENCES.
E. J. EVANS, FAMILY GROCER, SOUTH STREET, LEOMINSTER.

Left: *Edward Juson Evans established his successful photographic business in the early 1860s at No.36 South Street. He was certainly there in 1867 and remained there until his move to No.22 Burgess Street in 1890. A lifelong Baptist, he sold his business to Alfred De'Ath on his retirement in 1905.*

Brace the Blacksmith

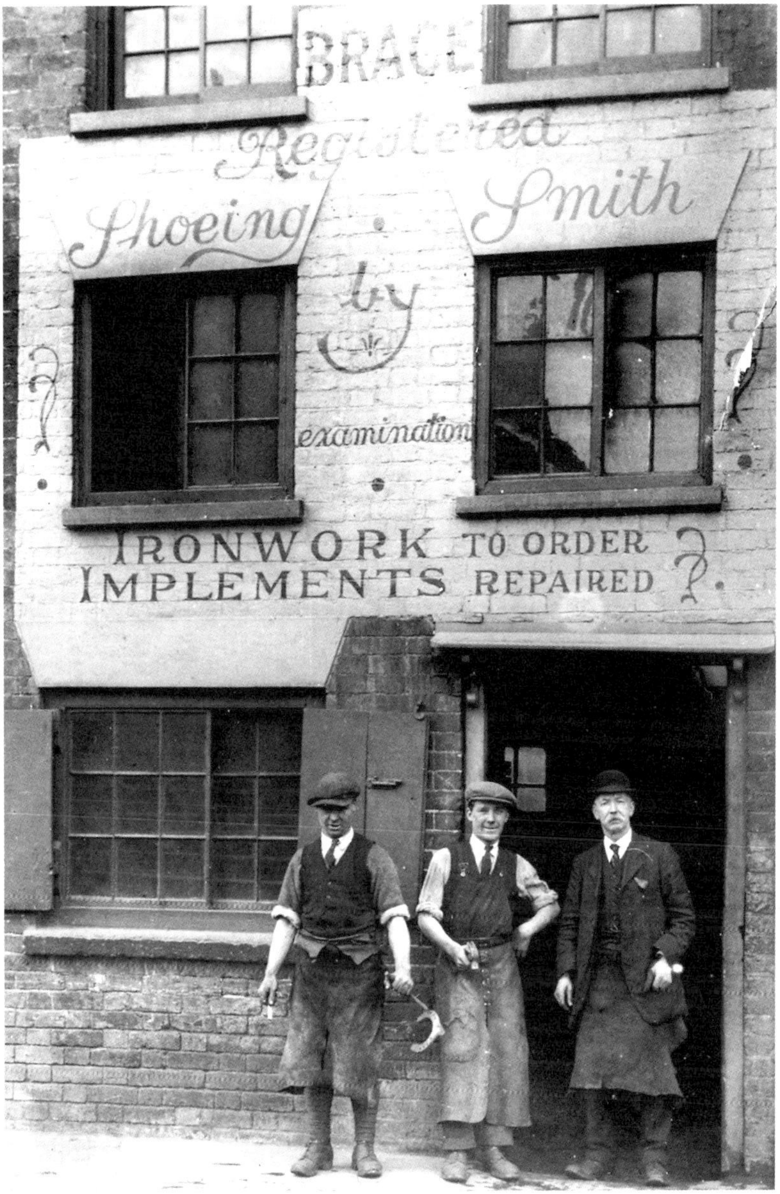

For over 37 years, from 1890 to 1926, James Brace owned blacksmith's premises at No.39 Broad Street and No.27 South Street near the Iron Cross, where he poses with two of his farriers in 1908; he later moved to No.49 South Street. In 1919 the cost of shoeing a cob or pony was seven shillings; a heavy carthorse ten shillings; and (as it did not involve the cost of materials) removing shoes was half price. Like many other blacksmiths he was ready to take on jobs making or repairing anything made of iron.

James Fryer's Garage

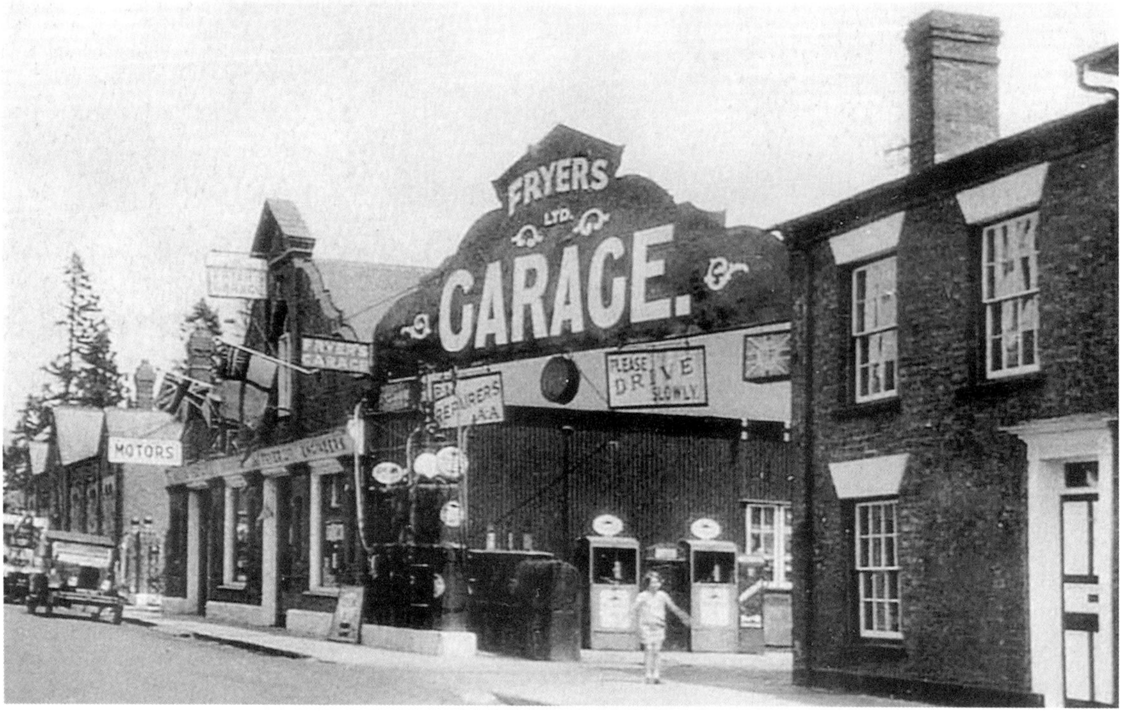

Above: *As an astute businessman, James Fryer soon realised the potential of making money from the newly-arrived motor car, and established a garage in South Street in 1908/9. In this 1938 photograph, long before self-service was thought of, an attendant had to swing a long boom from the petrol pump across the pavement to refuel cars. A little girl skips along the pavement in front of two cabinets containing engine oil. The purpose-built car showrooms fronted the street with the workshops to the rear. Now demolished, Fryer's impressive building has became the car park for the British Legion hall. The Friends Meeting House – the building on the left of the garage – changed ownership in 1975 and has since become a night-club. Since this photograph was taken, the house on the right has been considerably modified.*

Right: *A 1924 bill from James Fryer Ltd. for 28s. 'for a drive gear ball bearing for an Essex car'.*

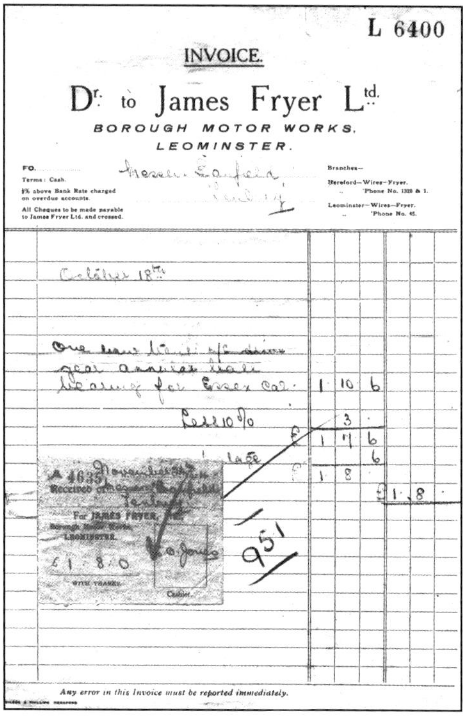
L 6400

INVOICE.

Dr. to James Fryer Ltd.

BOROUGH MOTOR WORKS,

LEOMINSTER.

FO.

Terms: Cash.

½% above Bank Rate charged on overdue accounts.

All Cheques to be made payable to James Fryer Ltd. and crossed.

Branches—

Hereford—Wires—Fryer. 'Phone No. 1320 & 1.

Leominster—Wires—Fryer. 'Phone No. 45.

October 18th

Less 10%

For JAMES FRYER,

Borough Motor Works,

LEOMINSTER.

WITH THANKS.

Cashier.

Any error in this Invoice must be reported immediately.

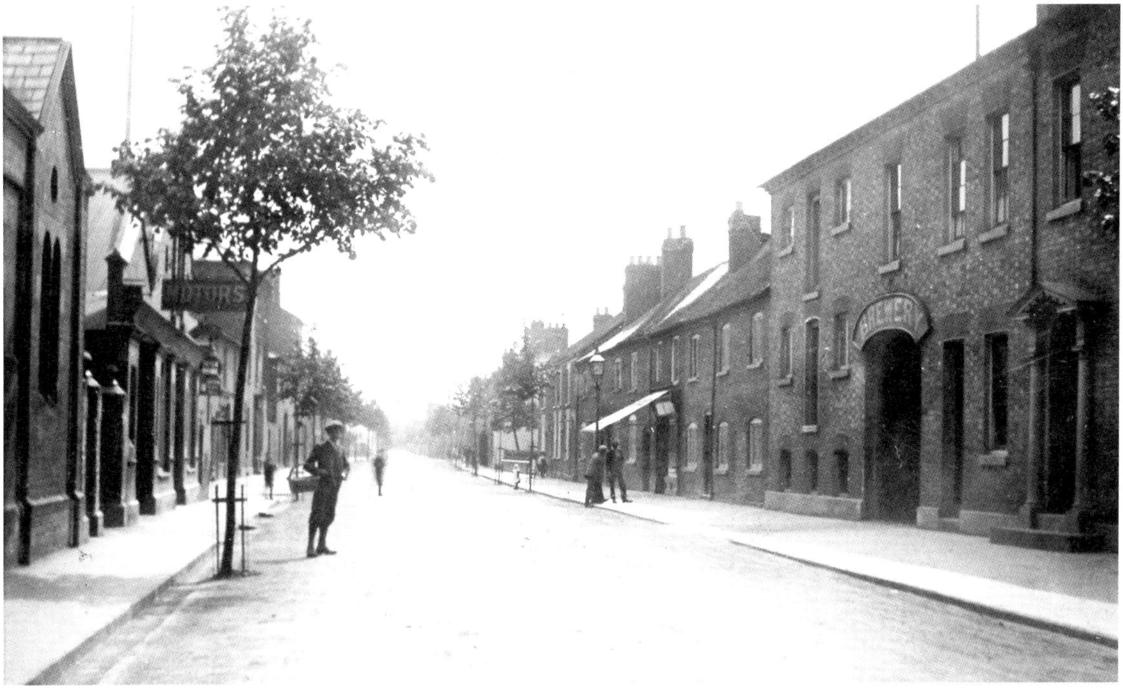

Above: *Looking south down a traffic-free South Street in 1911, still lined with the trees planted some 30 years earlier.*

From the profits of his other businesses Charles Blundell built the Britannia Brewery (on the right of the photograph) at No.44 South Street in the early 1870s. Competition between breweries must have been stiff and apparently it was a poor business proposition as it changed hands repeatedly. By 1892 Wilmot and Co. had re-named it simply 'The Brewery'. Continued competition must have faced Alexander McNish, who had taken it over in 1902, renaming it the 'Leominster Brewery', from where he also sold wines and spirits. Ownership changed again in 1904 when Paxton and Co. were advertising their products in the Leominster News. *Now modernised and altered, the building is still recognisable, though the cottages beyond it have been replaced with the entrance to Hawthorn Drive.*

PAGE and SON,
BUILDERS & CONTRACTORS,
South Street, LEOMINSTER.

ESTIMATES GIVEN FOR GENERAL REPAIRS.

Left: *Page and Son were general builders in Leominster for many years. Their yard was some distance from the centre of the town at No.114 South Street.*

Newlands

As Leominster began to spread outwards in the twentieth century, the higher ground at Newlands, to the south west, offered an attractive housing area. Rural lanes and picturesque walks were transformed out of recognition by much needed houses.

Right: *Newlands Croft, standing on the quiet corner of Newlands and Ryefield Roads in about 1920.*

Below: *Full of colour in springtime, this pretty Cyclamen Walk led to a Swiss-type Chalet at Newlands. The whole area is now changed out of all recognition and is covered in modern housing.*

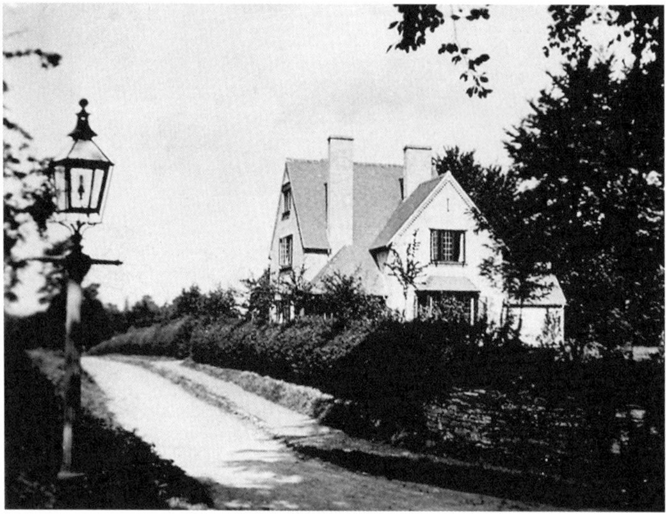

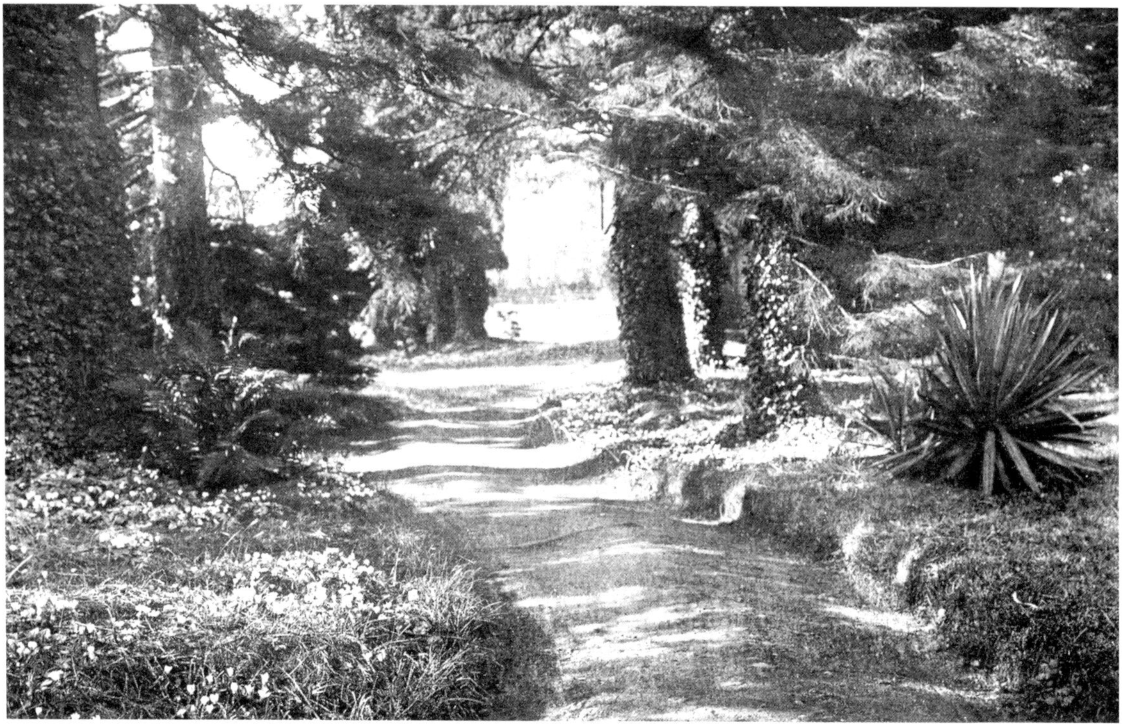

People, Trades and Events

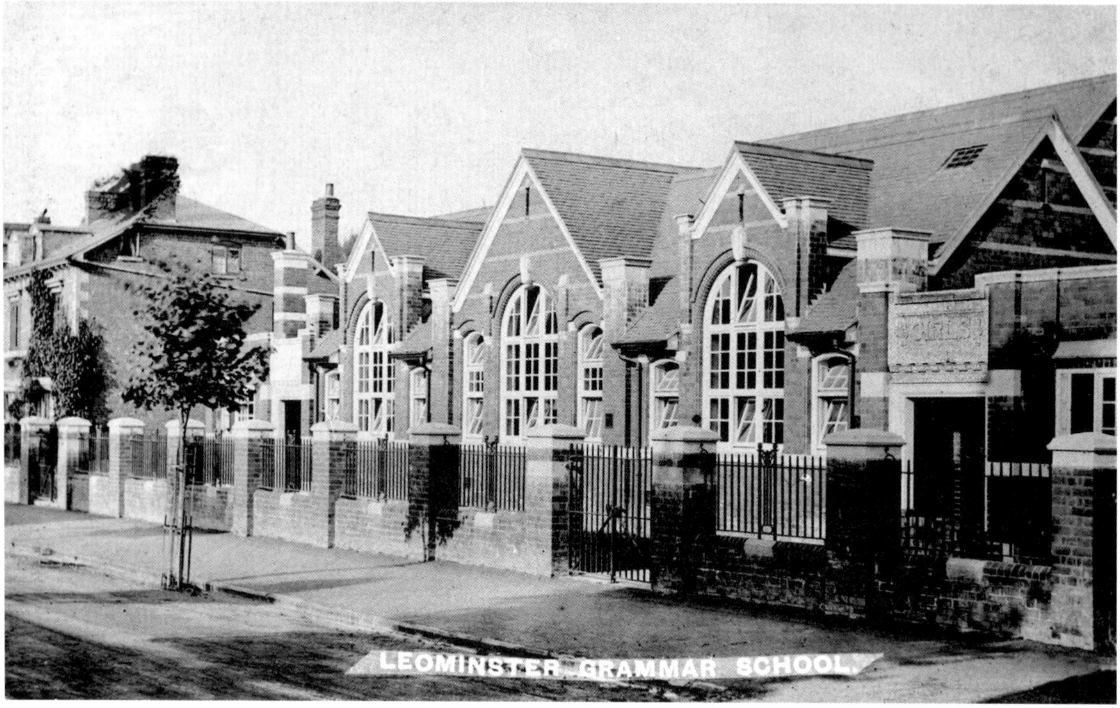

The iron gates and railings have disappeared in the century since its erection and as a sign of the equality of the sexes the words BOYS and GIRLS over their original separate doorways have been removed from the now renamed Minster College.

The School

In 1908 Herefordshire County Education Committee, under the dominating influence of its chairman, Sir James Rankin, offered £2,750 towards the construction of a Secondary School in Leominster if the Town Council would find the remainder. It appears that Rankin, an astute politician who was temporarily out of Parliament, had an eye on re-election and wanted to sweeten the local electorate.

A local builder, J.H. Davies of the Vinery, was awarded the contract for the building work for £3,542, which he successfully kept within budget. Fully equipped, Leominster Secondary School cost just over £4,000. Grants from the Board of Education helped with the running costs. William St.George Drennan M.Sc., from Selby in Yorkshire, was the successful candidate from over two hundred applicants for the job as its first headmaster. With a starting salary of £300 he was given an incentive to succeed with a capitation allowance of £2 for every pupil in excess of 50. He gave the town and the school yeoman service for the 21 years he remained headmaster.

The opening ceremony took place at the Town Hall on 30 September 1909, where Rankin was presented with a gold key as a memento. 56 boys and girls paying £2 per term and 19 free pupils started school the next day. Books cost another ten shillings per term. Under Drennan's energetic guidance, however, pupil numbers soared to 160 so rapidly that in 1912 a new lecture room, a science laboratory, two art rooms, a cookery room for girls and a manual labour room (for wood and metal work) for boys had to be built at a cost of £2,800. Numbers continued to rise to 185, enabling Drennan to achieve his dream when, on 1 April 1915, the school governors renamed it the Leominster Grammar School, a change which enabled it to attract more Government funding.

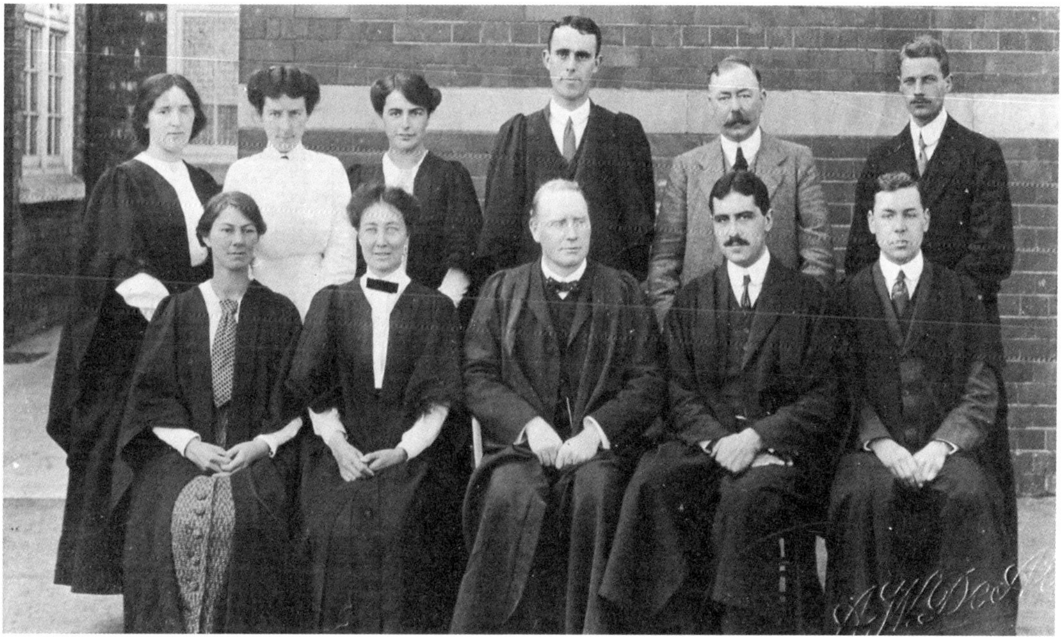

The headmaster with a group of his staff in about 1910, including Mr L.W. Leyland, Miss Gladys James, Miss L. Preece (art teacher), Miss Teresa Smith, and Miss F.E. Graham.

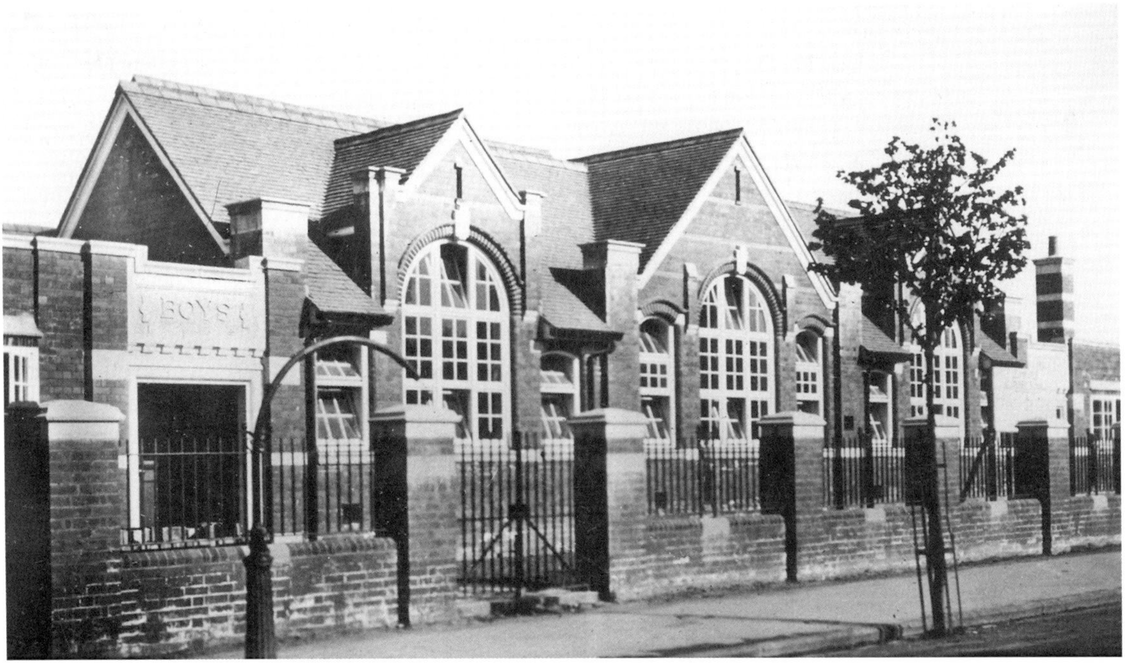

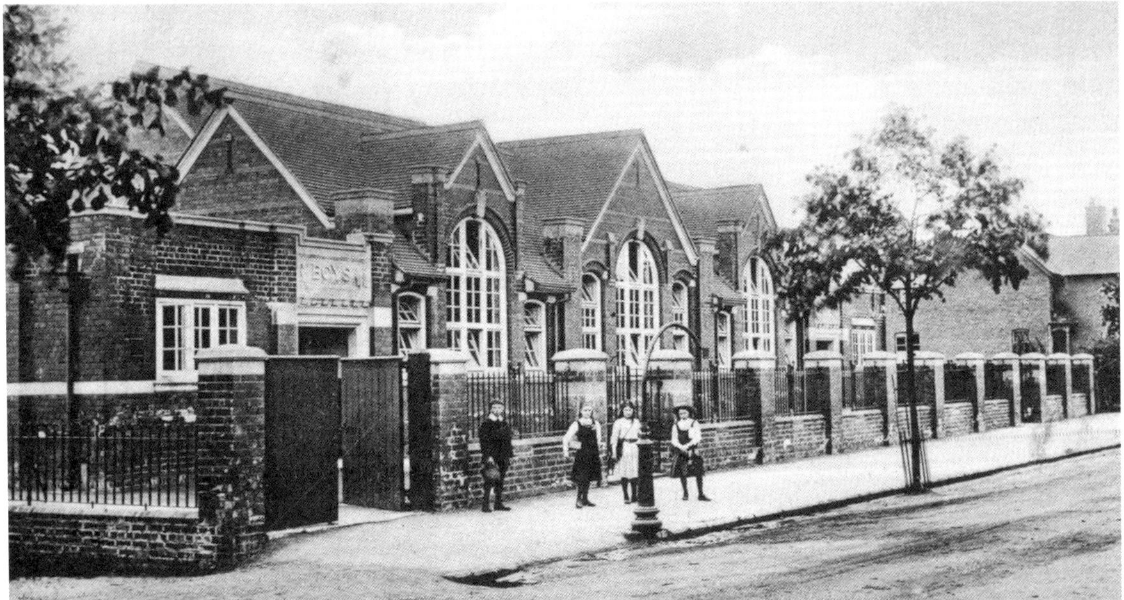

Two postcards of Leominster Secondary School in 1915 and 1924.

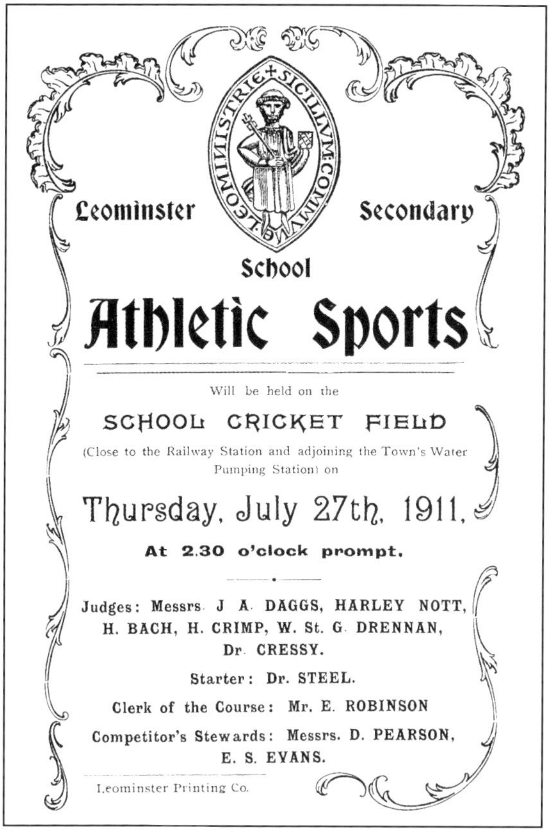

Leominster Secondary School

Athletic Sports

Will be held on the

SCHOOL CRICKET FIELD

(Close to the Railway Station and adjoining the Town's Water Pumping Station) on

Thursday, July 27th, 1911,

At 2.30 o'clock prompt.

Judges: Messrs. J. A. DAGGS, HARLEY NOTT, H. BACH, H. CRIMP, W. St. G. DRENNAN, Dr. CRESSY.

Starter: Dr. STEEL.

Clerk of the Course: Mr. E. ROBINSON

Competitor's Stewards: Messrs. D. PEARSON, E. S. EVANS.

Leominster Printing Co.

Left: *The athletic sports afternoon in 1911 was scheduled to last four hours on the cricket pitch near the railway station. Prizes for the winners of the 38 events included tennis racquets, silver brooches, fishing rods and baskets, watches, handkerchief boxes, stamp albums, a hockey stick, footballs, desks, a cycle lamp, a silver fountain pen, a cricket bat, pocket knife, camera, compendium of games, clock, needle case, handbag, etc., all donated by local shopkeepers or members of staff.*

Below: *With her head fashionably shaded from the sun by a huge floral hat, Lady Rankin, wife of the local M.P., presented the fortunate winners' prizes. Here a boy receives a fishing basket as reward for his efforts on the running track, as the headmaster, W.St.G. Drennan, watches with an approving smile.*

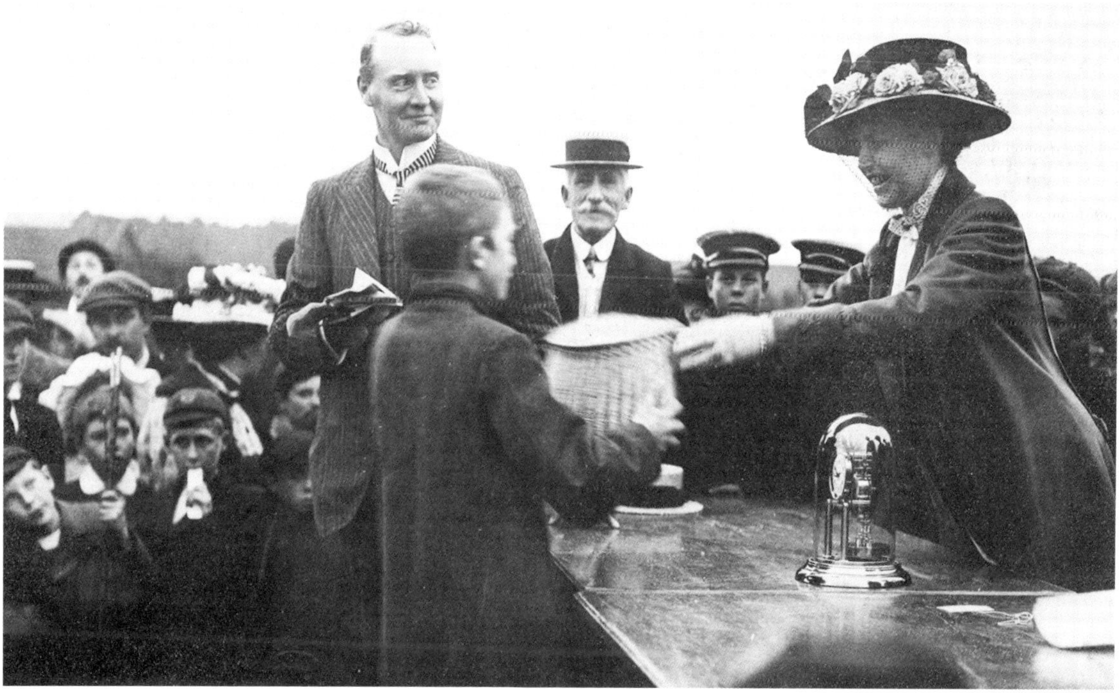

Access to a sports field was a problem from the time the school opened, when efforts to purchase the neighbouring fields failed. After protracted negotiations the school governors were eventually able to rent the land for £25 per annum, with the owner retaining his right to graze his sheep there at night, weekends and school holidays.

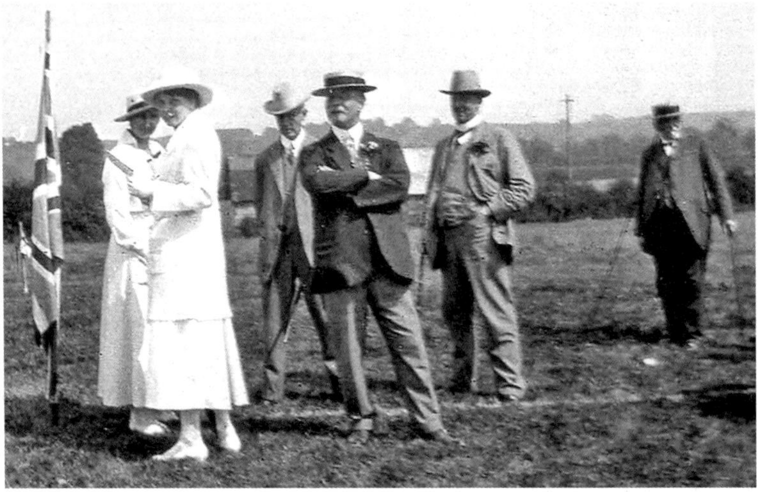

A scene of a wartime sports day in about 1917.

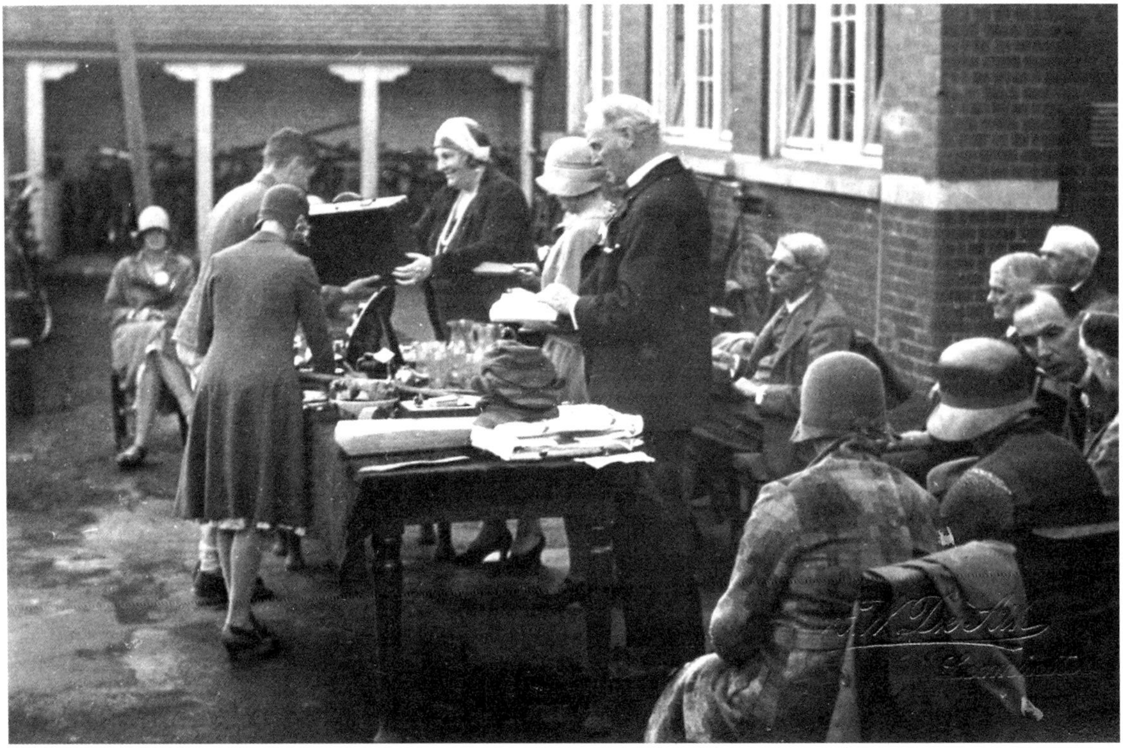

In the school playground a table laden with prizes awaits the winning athletes after another sports day in 1922 as fashionably dressed mothers watch the proceedings.

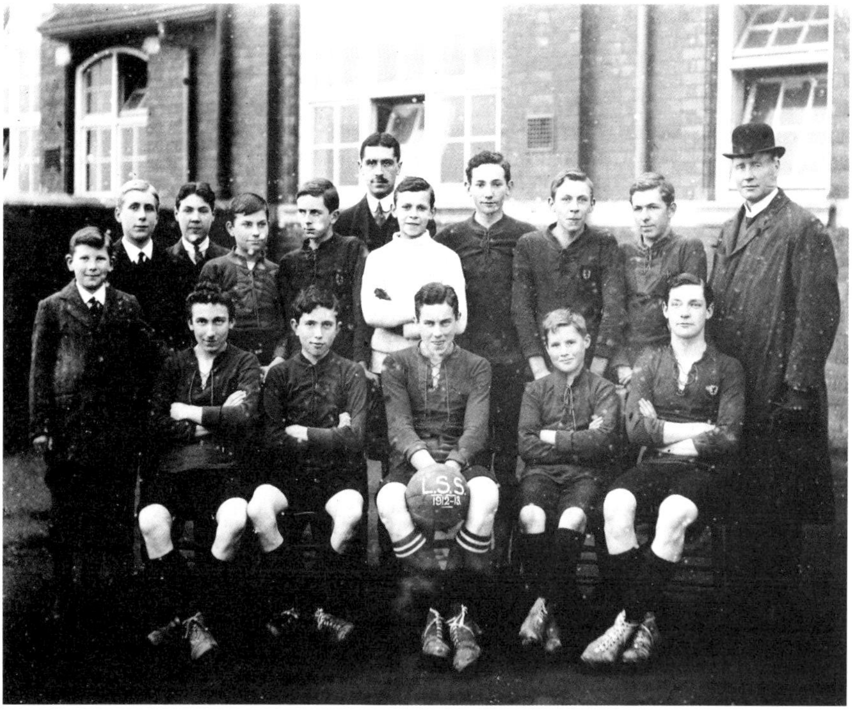

Left: *The Leominster Secondary School football team in the 1912–13 season.*

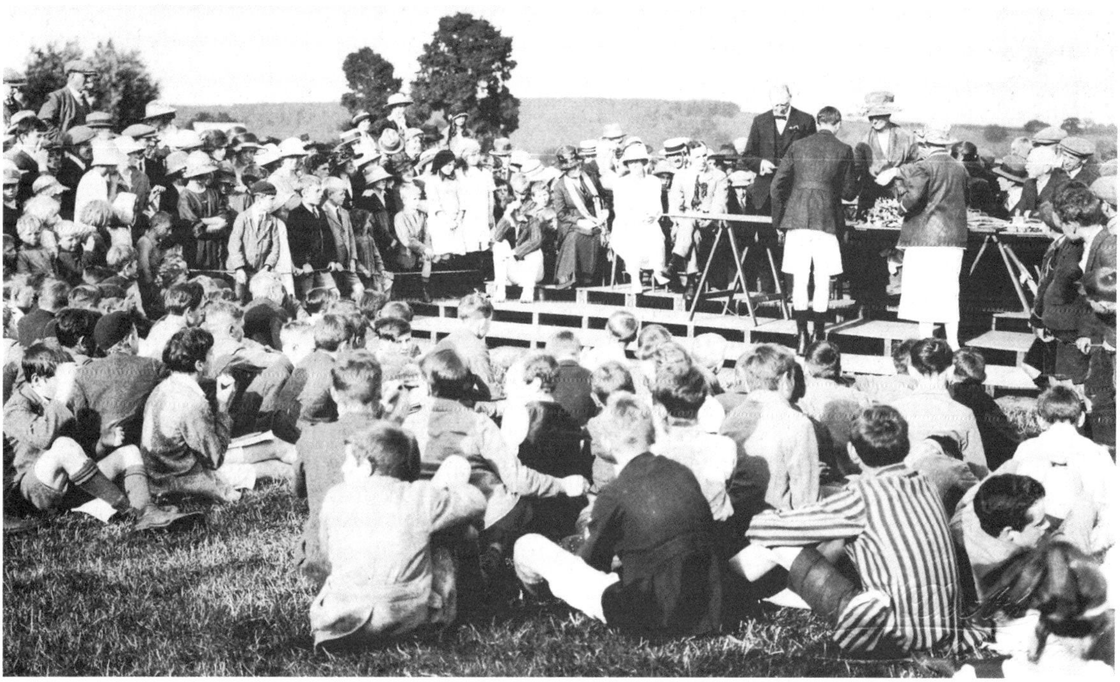

Children sit on the grass as their parents watch a prize giving ceremony on the cricket field in about 1925.

Right: *Headmaster Drennan posed with eleven members of the staff of the Grammar School in 1919. The photograph is believed to include W. Williams, W.G. Bisson, H. Adams, G.L. Lewis, E. Wright, A. Watson, W. Stone, Miss Roscoe, Miss Howells, Miss Taylor, and Miss Church.*

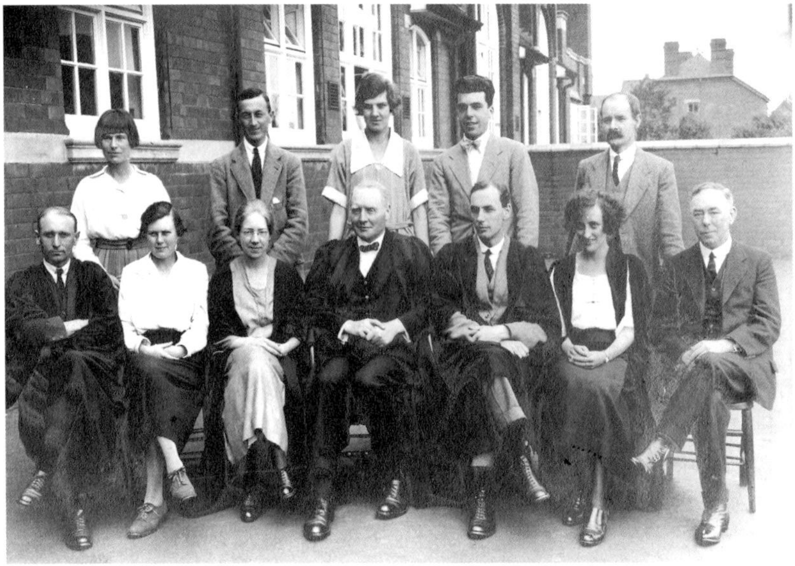

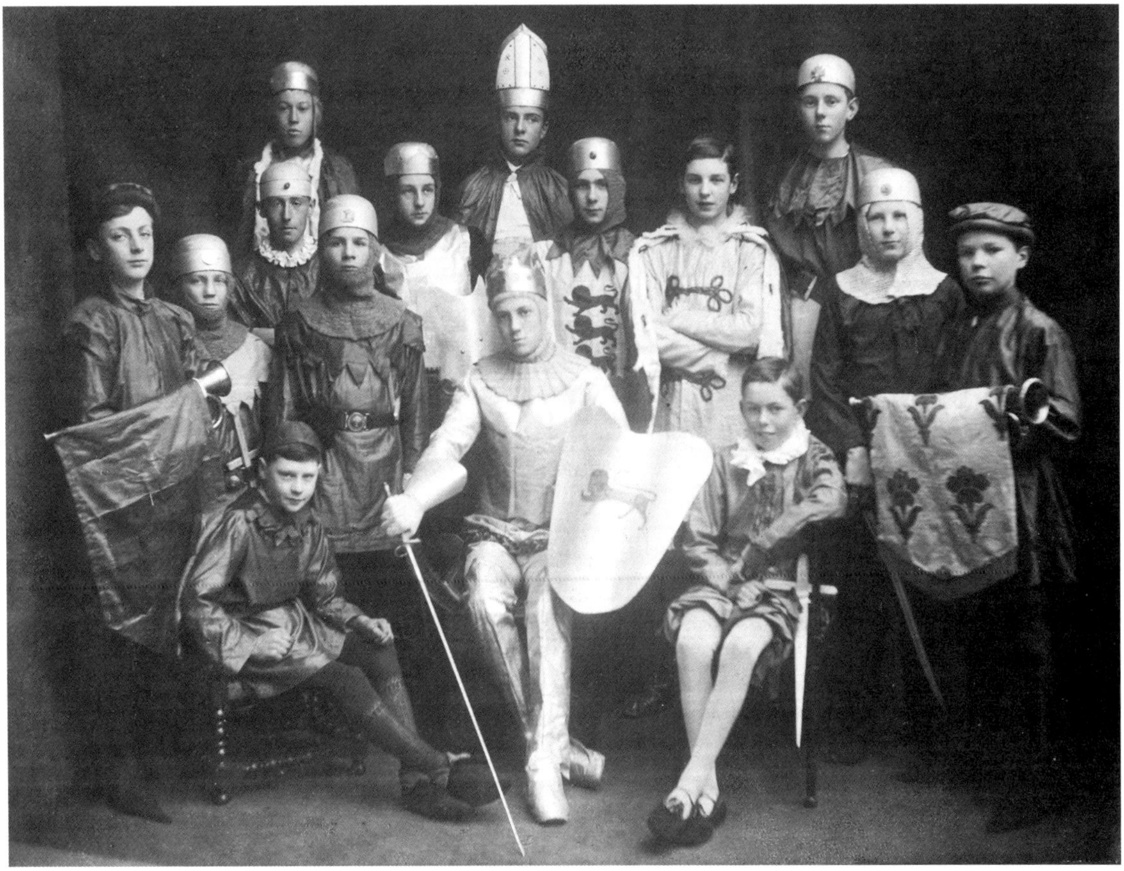

A schoolboys' production of Henry V.

Markets and Money

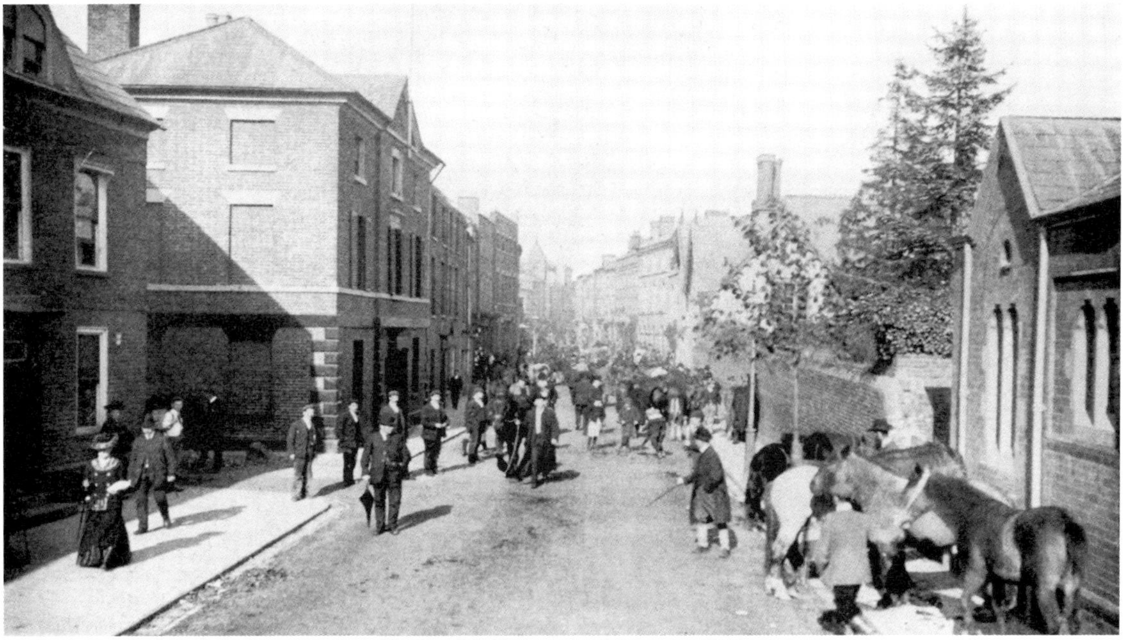

Above: *For centuries until well into the 1800s, when townspeople began to complain of the dirt and disturbance, Leominster's streets, especially Broad Street, were the recognised market places for animals from the district's fertile farms. Sheep were sold in Rainbow Lane, pigs in New Street, cattle in Dishley and West Streets, and horses in Etnam Street. However, at variance with information given in local Directories, this photograph shows a horse fair taking place in South Street about 1906 outside the Friends Meeting House on the right. The Essoldo Cinema, now a Bingo Hall, replaced the house opposite on the left.*

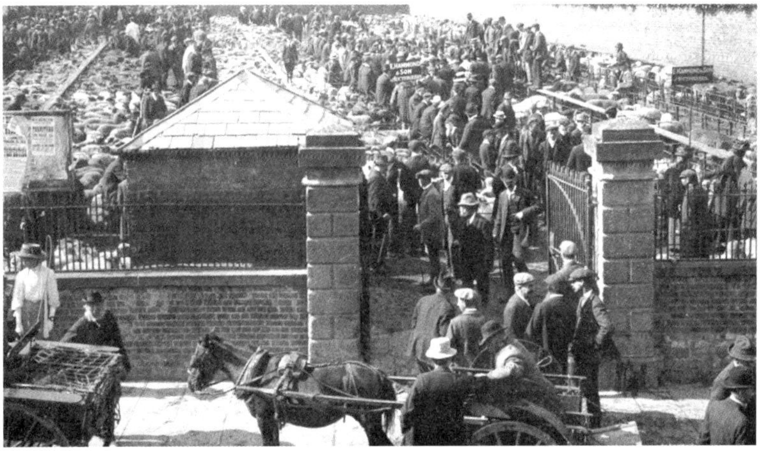

Left: *In 1808 a purpose-built pig and sheep market was constructed between Bargates and Rainbow Street, convenient to the town centre with this gateway opposite Hinton's store. The row of town houses opposite Hinton's old store has been built across this market entrance. Bengry's and Cursneh Road, the 1960s relief road, were built on much of the rest of the market site, where auctioneers, butchers and dealers once made comfortable livings from Herefordshire's livestock.*

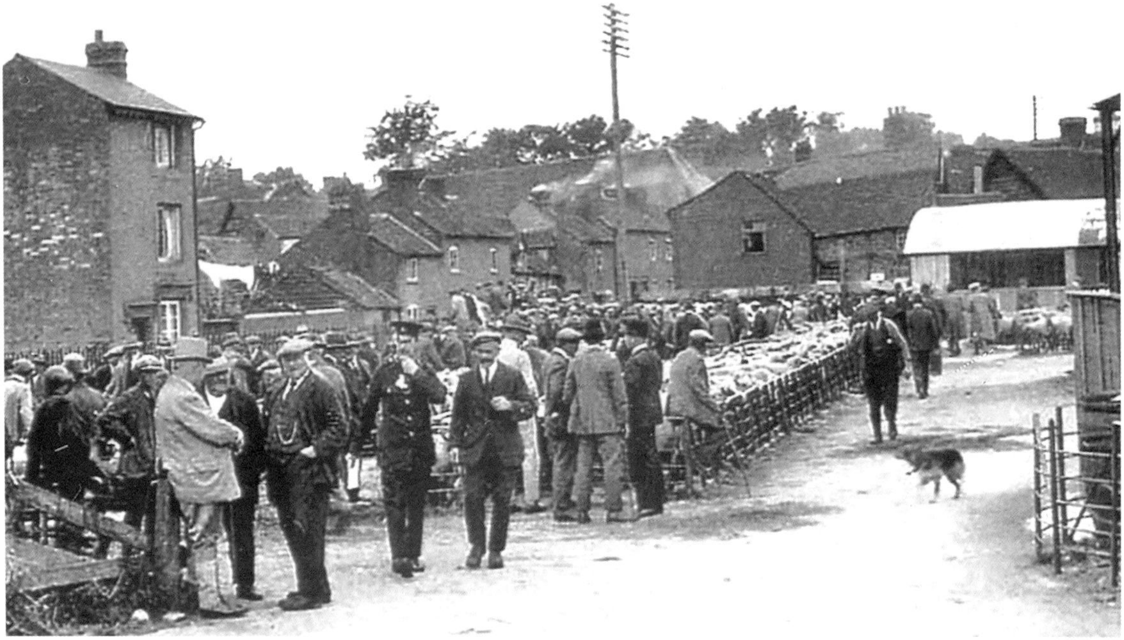

In 1908, the auctioneers Messrs. Cooper and Baldwin erected a cattle market in Dishley Street. A sheep and pig market already existed nearby between Bargates and Rainbow Street. By 1922 the firm of Edwards, Russell and Baldwin had taken over as auctioneers, estate agents, valuers and accountants, with premises in Hereford, Leominster and Tenbury.
This amateur photograph shows their packed sheep pens on a busy market day in 1938 as a group of farmers discuss the day's prices. The white corrugated iron building on the right was George Foster's wool, corn, seed and fodder merchant's warehouse. In 1941 he advertised as being a dog and poultry food specialist, operating from his other premises at Marsh (or Porter's) Mill. With modern redevelopments of the whole area, these sheep pens have become the service entrance to the rear of Somerfield supermarket. Foster's animal feed warehouse is now used by Minster Windows and beside it the house with the unevenly-sloping roof is a funeral directors premises. The decrepit houses in Dishley Street on the left were included in a slum clearance scheme and were demolished to make way for the busy ring road, where a continual stream of cars now queue at the Bargates junction traffic lights.

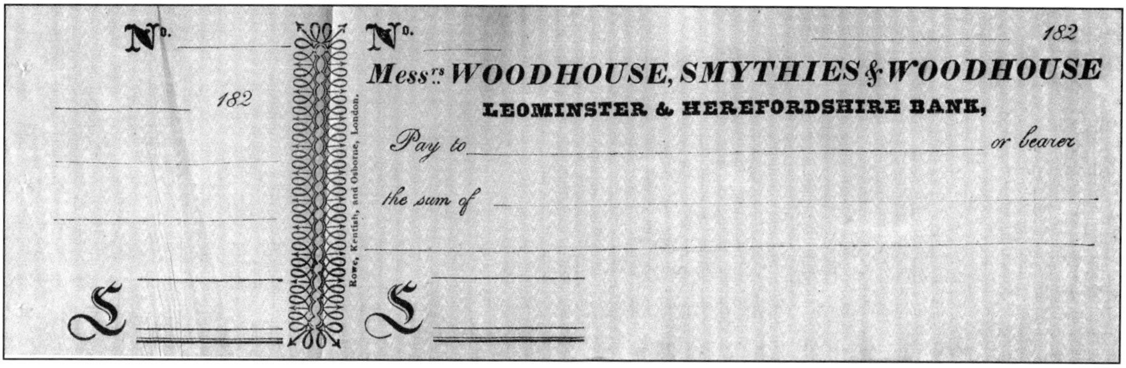
No.

182

No. 182

Mess.rs WOODHOUSE, SMYTHIES & WOODHOUSE

LEOMINSTER & HEREFORDSHIRE BANK,

Pay to ______ or bearer

the sum of ______

£

Rowe, Kentish, and Osborne, London.

£

Above: *Apart from the appearance of account and security numbers, the wording, layout and design of bank cheques has scarcely changed since their introduction 200 years ago. It is shown by this 1828 survivor of Woodhouse, Smythes and Woodhouse's Leominster and Hereford Bank. Every item of expense was immaculately entered into their account books, and although they dealt in thousands of pounds, minor costs like 2s. for sweeping chimneys, 3s. 6d. for cleaning the bank, and 7s. for a money shovel were all itemised. By 1835 these bankers seem to have retired, although from 1835 to 1851 Francis Woodhouse managed the Herefordshire Banking Company in Church Street.*

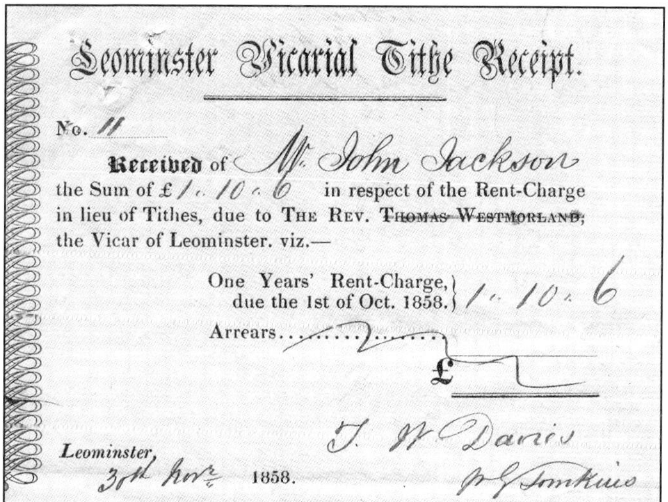
Leominster Vicarial Tithe Receipt.

No. 11

Received of Mr. John Jackson

the Sum of £ 1. 10. 6 in respect of the Rent-Charge in lieu of Tithes, due to The Rev. ~~Thomas Westmorland~~; the Vicar of Leominster. viz.—

One Years' Rent-Charge, due the 1st of Oct. 1858. 1. 10. 6

Arrears......

£

Leominster, 30th Nov. 1858.

T. W. Davis

W. G. Tomkins

Right: *At the height of its powers in medieval times, the Church charged land owners and occupiers a tithe, originally one tenth of the land's produce. The few huge surviving tithe barns show that this was paid in actual produce. Later, as coins became more freely available, the church accepted money in lieu. As time elapsed the system changed and tithes could be bought and sold (like shares) or commuted to rent charges. Across the country, many thought that abuses occurred and that the charges were excessive. The system came under increasing attack as being unfair, especially when Nonconformists and others with different beliefs to the Church of England objected to paying towards the upkeep of churches they did not attend or for ministers whose beliefs were contrary to their own. So strong was the Church of England's position in the establishment that the archaic system survived into the twentieth century. Illustrated is a 1858 Vicarial Tithe receipt for £1 10s. from John Jackson, a farmer residing at Colaba Lodge.*

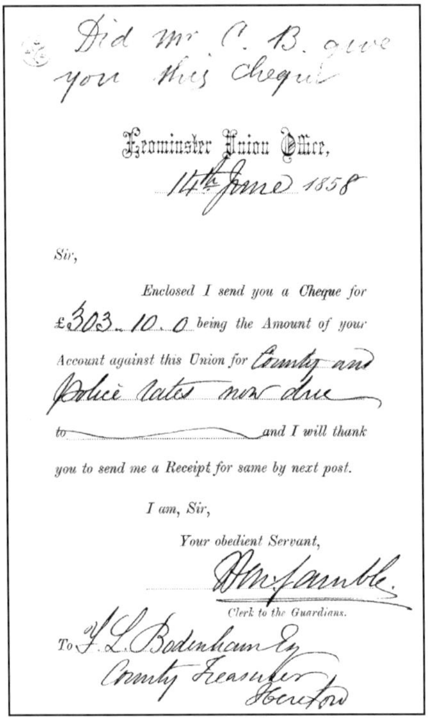

Did Mr C. B. give you this Cheque

Leominster Union Office,

14th June 1858

Sir,

Enclosed I send you a Cheque for £303. 10. 0 being the Amount of your Account against this Union for County and Police rates now due to ―――――― and I will thank you to send me a Receipt for same by next post.

I am, Sir,

Your obedient Servant,

[signature]

Clerk to the Guardians.

To J. L. Bodenham Esq
County Treasurer
Hereford

Left: *The Leominster Union responsible for the administration of the Poor Law was not immune from the county rating system, as this 1858 covering letter for county and police rates of £303 10s. shows.*

Below: *The three pence demanded from Mr Drennan in 1918 by Leominster Union for Poor Relief may well have cost more than this to collect.*

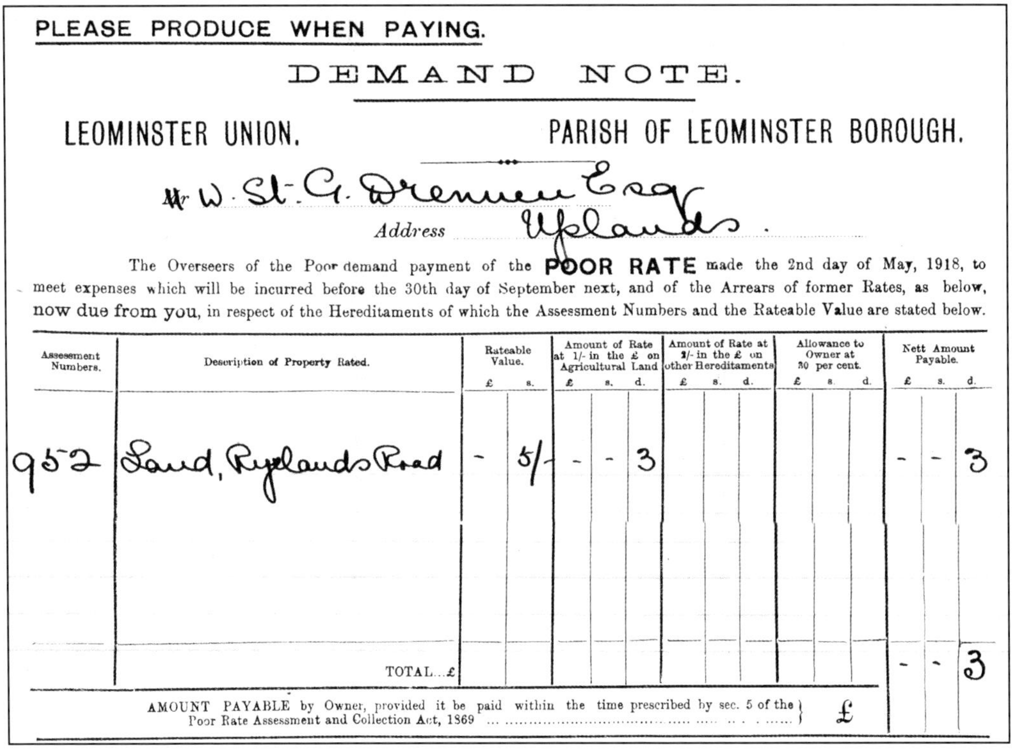

PLEASE PRODUCE WHEN PAYING.

DEMAND NOTE.

LEOMINSTER UNION. PARISH OF LEOMINSTER BOROUGH.

Mr W. St. G. Drennan Esq

Address Uplands.

The Overseers of the Poor demand payment of the **POOR RATE** made the 2nd day of May, 1918, to meet expenses which will be incurred before the 30th day of September next, and of the Arrears of former Rates, as below, now due from you, in respect of the Hereditaments of which the Assessment Numbers and the Rateable Value are stated below.

Assessment Numbers.	Description of Property Rated.	Rateable Value. £	s.	Amount of Rate at 1/- in the £ on Agricultural Land £	s.	d.	Amount of Rate at 1/- in the £ on other Hereditaments £	s.	d.	Allowance to Owner at 30 per cent. £	s.	d.	Nett Amount Payable. £	s.	d.
952	Land, Rylands Road	-	5/-	-	-	3							-	-	3
	TOTAL...£												-	-	3

AMOUNT PAYABLE by Owner, provided it be paid within the time prescribed by sec. 5 of the Poor Rate Assessment and Collection Act, 1869 .... £

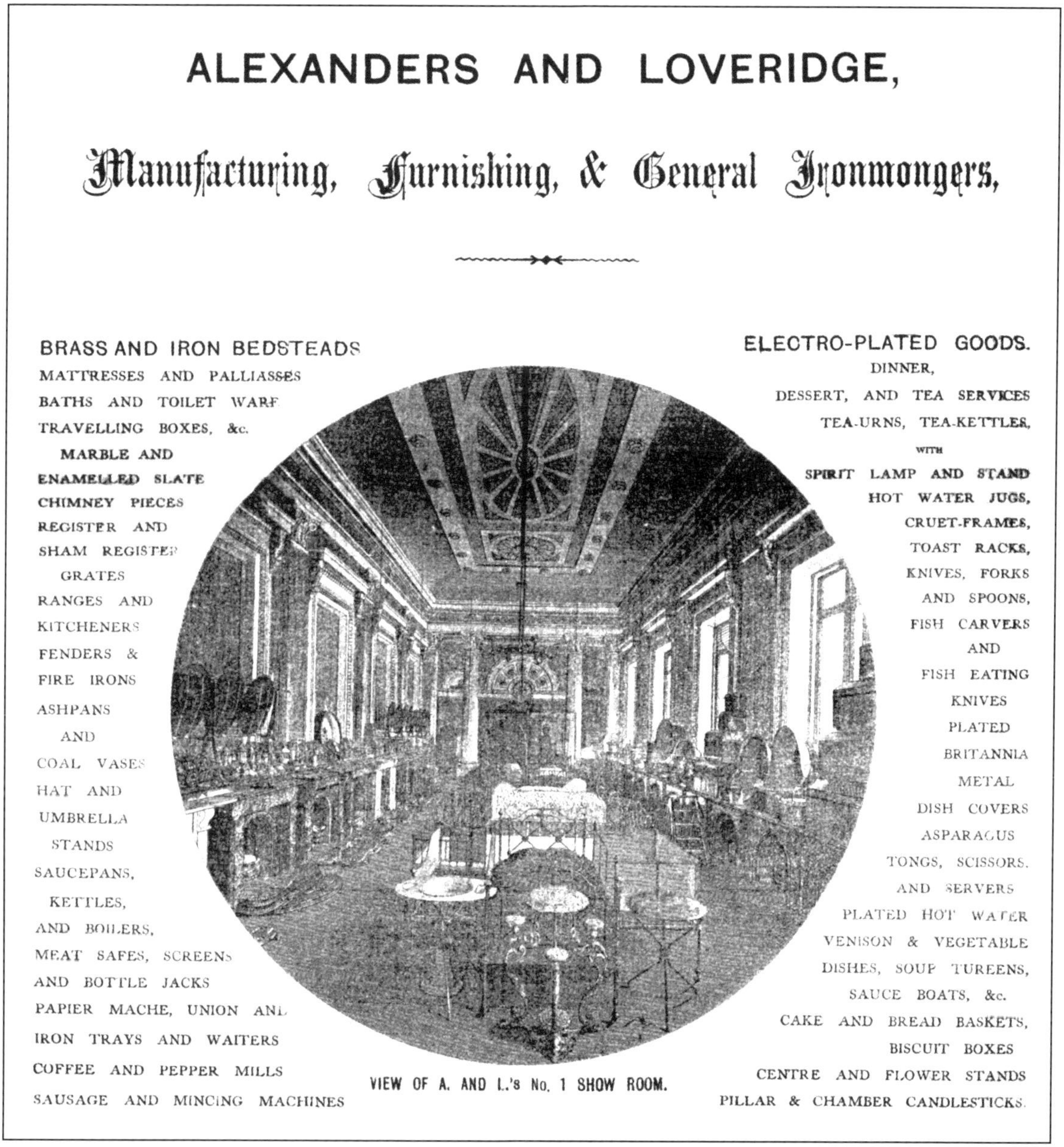

From contemporary advertisements it appears that Samuel Alexander established his ironmongery businesses in Corn Square and Broad Street in the 1850s. Certainly by 1859 he was selling a wide range of agricultural and household goods, competing for trade with a number of other shops, agencies, foundries and blacksmiths in the town.

In 1861 Samuel Alexander bought the Lion, a former coaching hotel in Broad Street, which had lost trade after the railway arrived in 1853. By 1864 he had moved all his businesses into these spacious premises, converting the rooms fronting the street into offices and salesrooms, and the old stable yard at the rear into a factory. In 1870, feeling the effects of advancing age, he restructured the firm as a partnership between his two sons and his promising apprentice, Thomas Loveridge. About this time the firm started to use the Lion Ballroom to display their household ironmongery, as the advertisement in Littlebury's 1876 *Directory* on the previous page shows.

On his father's death in 1886, Samuel Alexander bought out Loveridge's interest in the firm and entered a long-lasting and very successful partnership with Andrew Duncan, another one-time apprentice. Under their leadership, the Lion Works prospered and expanded as much as its now cramped space allowed. They became the largest employer in Leominster, and their salesmen were kept busy on market days in Hereford and Tenbury taking orders for their own agricultural machinery as well as for other manufacturers for which they were agents. Another speciality was their steel-framed Dutch barns, roofed with corrugated iron, for storing hay and straw, many of which can still be seen on farms in the area. Other corrugated iron structures were designed for use by impecunious religious groups – these buildings often being referred to as 'tin tabernacles'.

Expecting an increase in trade after the First World War, they made one of their few mistakes and stocked Birmingham-built Garner tractors. Priced at £385, they were well above the cost of their competitors' more affordable Fordsons. After weathering this mistake they concentrated on their agricultural market and took a franchise for John Deere tractors, moving in 1975 to new premises in Southern Way.

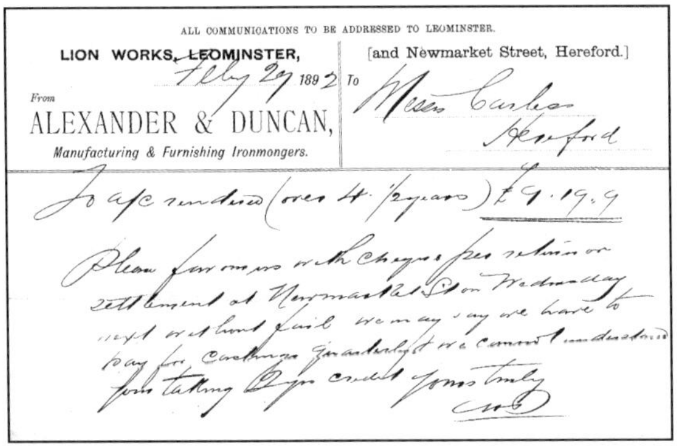

ALL COMMUNICATIONS TO BE ADDRESSED TO LEOMINSTER.

LION WORKS, ~~LEOMINSTER~~, [and Newmarket Street, Hereford.]

Feby 29 1892

To Messrs Carless, Hereford

From ALEXANDER & DUNCAN, Manufacturing & Furnishing Ironmongers.

To a/c rendered (over 4 1/2 years) £9.19.9

[illegible]

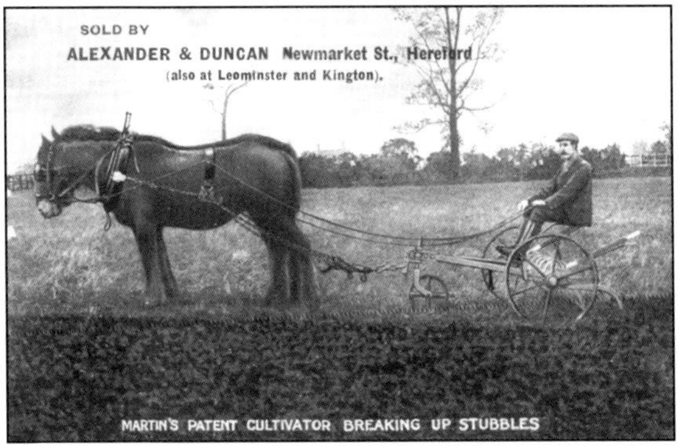

Above left: *The firm was financially secure and could allow credit of more than four years on a bill for £9 19s. 9d. as this 1892 reminder for payment shows.*

Above right: *Alexander and Duncan overprinted this 1913 advertising postcard for Martin cultivators to promote their business, which by this time had expanded into Hereford and Kington.*

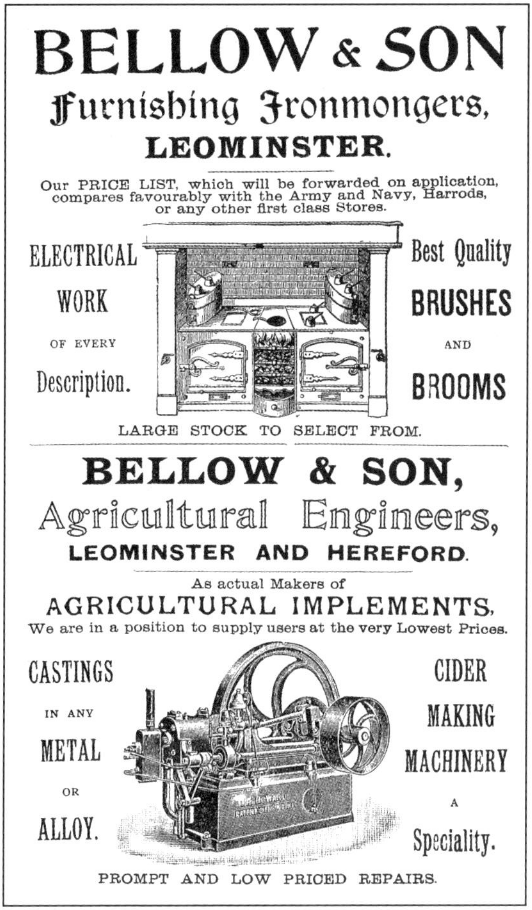

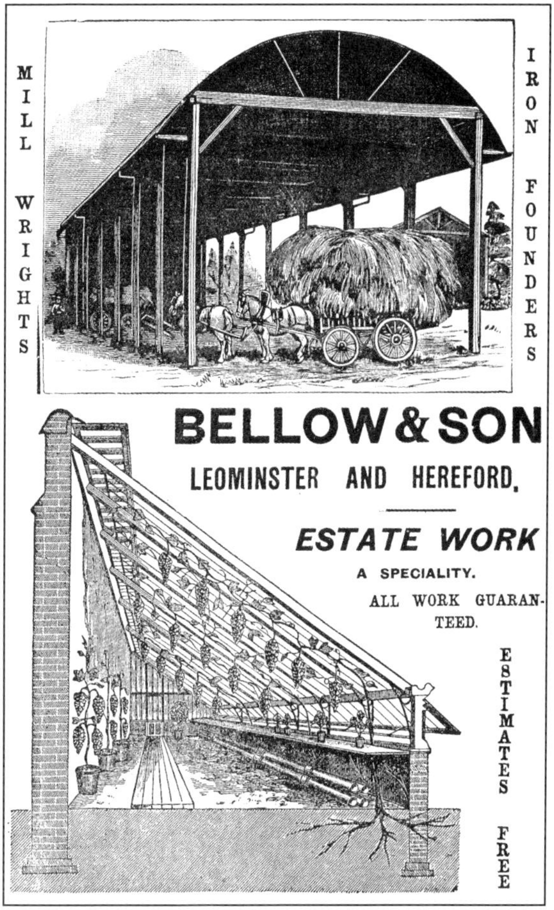

Since at least 1876 Bellows had been in competition with Alexander and Duncan and seemed to expand in step with them, even opening stores in Tenbury, Bromyard and Hereford. Thrifty farmers could shop around to find which firm would give them the best bargain. In 1919 Bellows were agents for Austin tractors. These advertisements appeared in Jakeman and Carver's 1902 Directory.

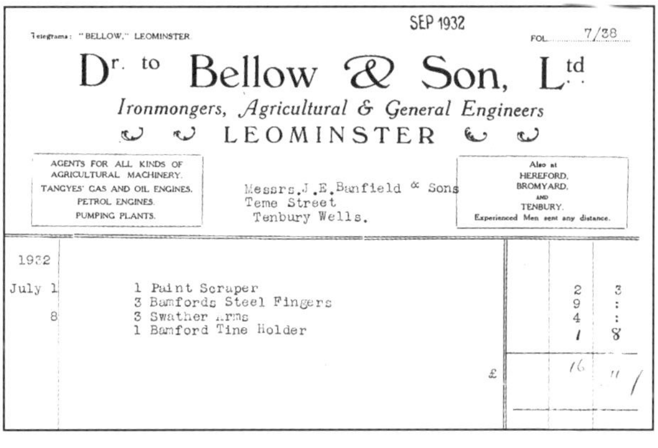

SEP 1932

Telegrams: "BELLOW," LEOMINSTER.

FOL. 7/38

Dr. to Bellow & Son, Ltd.

Ironmongers, Agricultural & General Engineers

LEOMINSTER

AGENTS FOR ALL KINDS OF AGRICULTURAL MACHINERY.
TANGYES' GAS AND OIL ENGINES.
PETROL ENGINES.
PUMPING PLANTS.

Messrs.J.E.Banfield & Sons
Teme Street
Tenbury Wells.

Also at
HEREFORD,
BROMYARD,
AND
TENBURY.
Experienced Men sent any distance.

1932			
July 1	1 Paint Scraper	2	3
	3 Bamfords Steel Fingers	9	:
8	3 Swather Arms	4	:
	1 Bamford Tine Holder	1	8
	£	16	" 1

Left: A Bellows and Son 1932 invoice. After this date they concentrated on the domestic market, but by 1950 the firm had disappeared from Leominster.

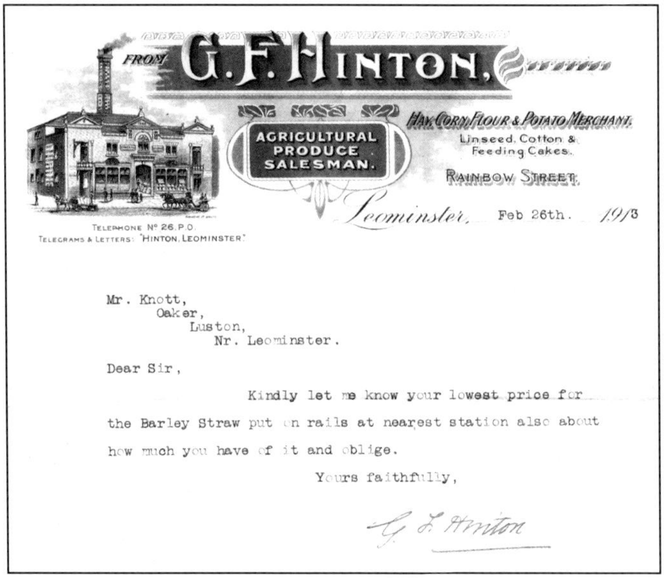

FROM G.F. HINTON,

AGRICULTURAL PRODUCE SALESMAN.

HAY, CORN, FLOUR & POTATO MERCHANT.
Linseed, Cotton & Feeding Cakes.

RAINBOW STREET.

Leominster, Feb 26th. 1913

TELEPHONE Nº 26. P.O.
TELEGRAMS & LETTERS: "HINTON, LEOMINSTER."

Mr. Knott,
Oaker,
Luston,
Nr. Leominster.

Dear Sir,

Kindly let me know your lowest price for the Barley Straw put on rails at nearest station also about how much you have of it and oblige.

Yours faithfully,

G. F. Hinton

Top: *Though their retail premises are now in Broad Street, George Hinton's original imposing brick shop-front facing Rainbow Street is still instantly recognisable from this 1913 letter heading. At that time he supplied fertilizers, sprays and animal feeds to the surrounding farmers who brought their pigs and sheep to the market opposite his shop. Hinton also owned another business in nearby West Street – a bakery and confectionery. Like other ambitious men he tried other businesses and in 1919 advertised his services as an auctioneer and general salesman.*

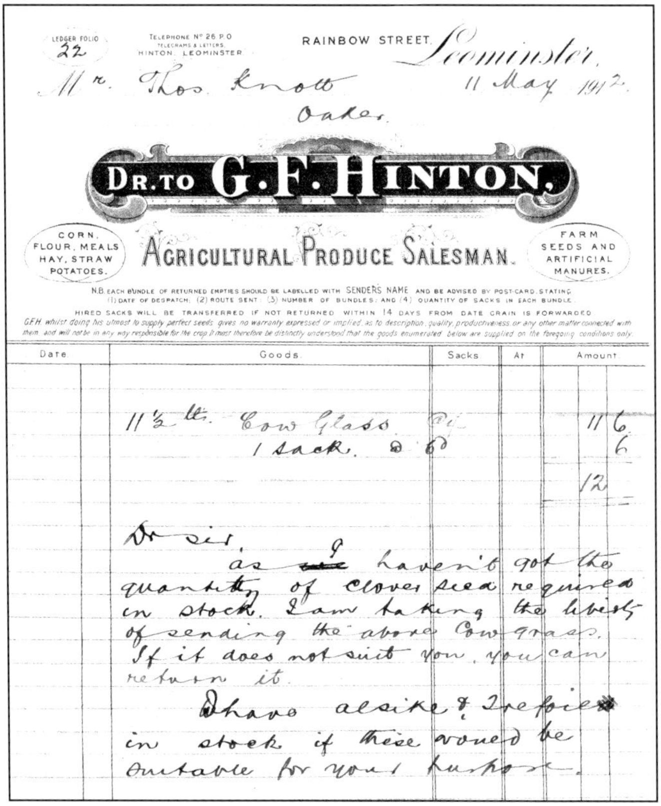

LEDGER FOLIO 22

TELEPHONE Nº 26 P.O.
TELEGRAMS & LETTERS.
HINTON, LEOMINSTER

RAINBOW STREET, Leominster,

Mr. Thos. Knott 11 May 1912.
Oaker.

DR. TO G.F. HINTON,

CORN, FLOUR, MEALS HAY, STRAW POTATOES.

AGRICULTURAL PRODUCE SALESMAN.

FARM SEEDS AND ARTIFICIAL MANURES.

N.B. EACH BUNDLE OF RETURNED EMPTIES SHOULD BE LABELLED WITH SENDER'S NAME AND BE ADVISED BY POST-CARD, STATING (1) DATE OF DESPATCH; (2) ROUTE SENT; (3) NUMBER OF BUNDLES; AND (4) QUANTITY OF SACKS IN EACH BUNDLE.

HIRED SACKS WILL BE TRANSFERRED IF NOT RETURNED WITHIN 14 DAYS FROM DATE GRAIN IS FORWARDED.

G.F.H. whilst doing his utmost to supply perfect seeds gives no warranty expressed or implied, as to description, quality, productiveness, or any other matter connected with them, and will not be in any way responsible for the crop. It must therefore be distinctly understood that the goods enumerated below are supplied on the foregoing conditions only.

Date	Goods	Sacks	At	Amount
	11½ lb. Cow Grass @ 1/-			11 6
	1 sack. @ 6d			6
				12

Dr Sir,
as I haven't got the quantity of clover seed required in stock. I am taking the liberty of sending the above Cow grass. If it does not suit you, you can return it.
I have alsike & Trefoil in stock if these would be suitable for your purpose.

Left: *Willingness to provide what the customer wanted is shown on this account for 12 shillings for 11½lbs of grass seed sent to Mr Knott of Luston in May 1912. Astute business acumen in dealing in a wide range of goods for the agricultural as well as the town customer has made Hinton's a household word in Leominster.*

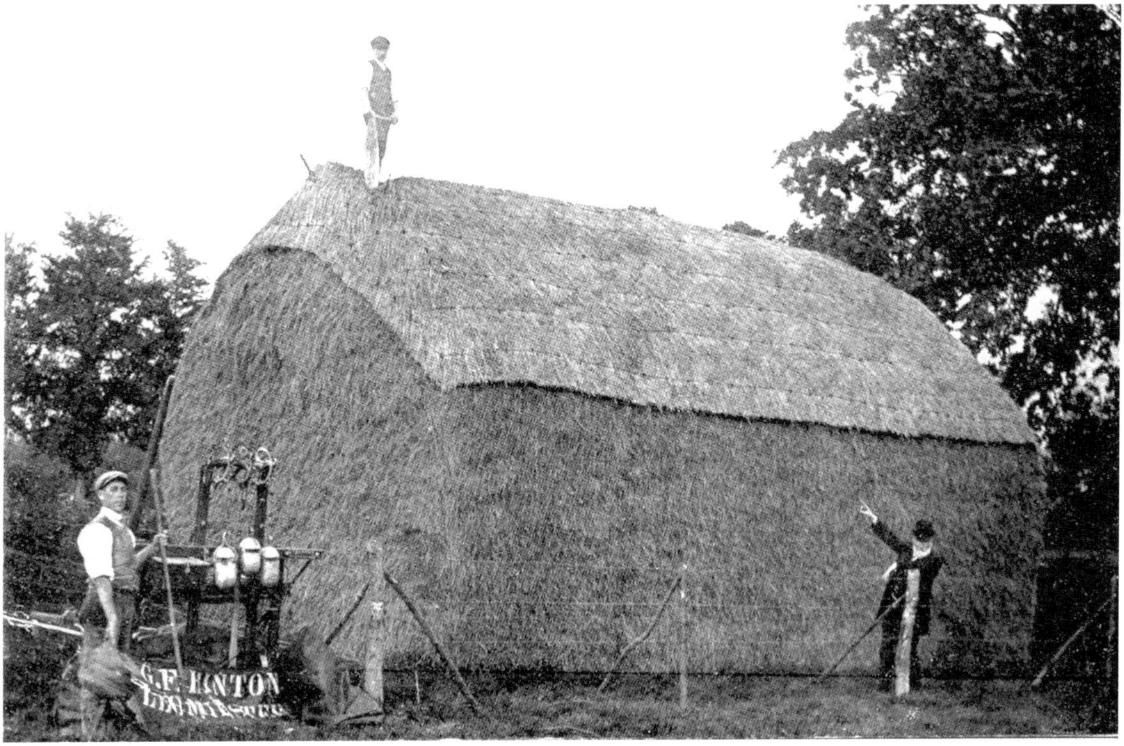

SEE ILLUSTRATION.

THIS STACK OF HAY weighed
16 Tons, 11 Cwts., 2 Qrs.
over Station Machine (668 TRUSSES, viz.:—665 Prime and 3 Inferior) off only 8 ACRES OF MEADOW LAND, dressed Two Years previously with
2 Tons of Bilston Basic Slag

Were the Stack in the Market now, it would make some **£82,** and rent of land is only £16 10s. which rent, of course, included an enormous crop of Aftermath, as rich, sweet and good as possible.

P.T.C.

Above and left: *George Hinton is seen on a promotional postcard for Bilston Basic Slag (a by-product of the iron smelting industry which was used as a grass fertilizer) pointing to a 16 ton stack of hay before his men started trussing it for sale. The man on the left has a primitive hay-trusser with which he and a co-worker probably took a week to do the job. During the centuries when horses were in use in towns, factories and mines, there was a ready all-year-round demand for good quality hay, which disappeared after the emergence of motor transport between the wars. After this huge demand for hay disappeared, a much greater acreage of farm land could be devoted to growing cereal and root crops. Surprisingly during the First World War, a greater tonnage of hay was sent to France to feed the army's horses than the tonnage of ammunition sent to feed the guns.*

G. F. HINTON,

Corn, Flour, Seed and Potato Merchant,

STORES: **Rainbow Street, Leominster.**

For Rapid Fattening and General Feeding of CATTLE and SHEEP

USE THE "ALBION" CAKES

AGENT FOR ***Basic Phosphate Powder***—A Cheap Manure of lasting character and well-proved merit; and ***Bernard and Algers'*** well-known Patent and other High-Class ***Manures.***

ALSO . . .

The Times Dining Rooms

AND

CONFECTIONERY STORES

8, West Street, LEOMINSTER.

PURE WHOLESOME BREAD.

QUALITY IS THE TEST OF CHEAPNESS.

Sole Agent for the Celebrated PURE "HANSA" YEAST.

Depot for the Unrivalled "MAZAWATTEE" CEYLON TEA.

Telegrams: "HINTON, LEOMINSTER."

THE STORES, LEOMINSTER,

January, 1898.

Dear Sir or Madam,

For some time past country journeys have been regularly taken to many of the places enumerated on the enclosed list.

I now extend the number, and solicit your valued orders.

The whole of my business has the very best personal supervision: I buy for prompt cash, and sell at a small profit.

Please fill in on attached Card particulars of goods required, and post it to reach here (if possible) one clear day before delivery.

Yours obediently,

G. F. HINTON.

PLAN OF DELIVERIES.

MONDAY.	TUESDAY.	WEDNESDAY.	THURSDAY.	FRIDAY.	SATURDAY.
Stoke	Ashton	Stretfordbury	Barons Cross	Blackpole	Barons Cross
Wickton	The Hundred	Hennor	Ebnal	Luston	Monkland
Humber	Middleton	Hamnish	Lawton	Eye	Stretford
Risbury	Little Hereford	Brockmanton	Eardisland	Moreton	Stockingfield
Pencombe	Wyson	Puddlestone	Hardwicke	Yarpole	Dilwyn
Broadfield	Brimfield	Hampton Charles	Bearwood	Bircher	The Haven
Bowla Lane	Stockton	Hatfield	Broxwood	Croft	Ivington
Steens Bridge	Kimbolton	Brierley	Pembridge	Orleton	Hyde Ash
Docklow	Grantsfield	Wharton	Kingsland	Eyton	Eyder Marsh
Grendon	Laysters	Ford Bridge	Mortimer's Cross	Aston	Aulden
Hampton Wafer		Marlbrook	Aymestrey	Lucton	Birley
Wacton		Newton	Yatton		Knapton
Bredenbury		Winsley	Wigmore		King's Pyon
Barons Cross		Hope	Lye—Upper & Lower		Weobley Marsh
Ebnal		Bodenham	Deerfold		Upper Hill
Cobnash			Bach Brook		Westhope Hill
Shirlheath			Covenhope		Bush Bank
Kingsland			Lingen		Canon Pyon
Shobdon					

Above: *Hinton's business reply postcard with his timetable for deliveries on the reverse.*

Left: *Hinton's advertisement from Jakeman and Carver's 1902* Directory.

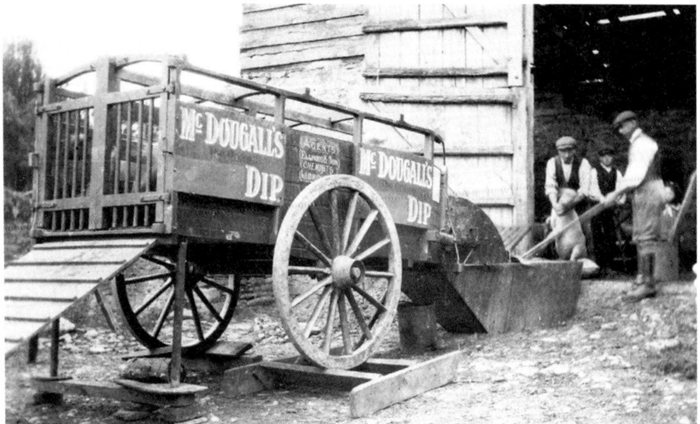

Right: *Farmers were required to dip their sheep on an annual basis to prevent sheep scab, and the local police force would visit farms to ensure that this had been done. Ellwood and Son were agents for McDougall's sheep dip solutions and hired a mobile dip to farmers who did not have dipping facilities of their own. In this photograph one man held a sheep ready to put in the dipping trough whilst another worker with a long pole pushed the sheep already in the trough under the chemical solution for a few seconds. The dipped sheep scrambled up the ramp to drip-dry in the sloping cart, from where any excess fluid ran back into the trough.*

Elections

Following the resignation of the Conservative M.P. Richard Arkwright, a by-election was held in 1875, at which Thomas Blake, a devout Baptist and businessman from Ross, was returned as Liberal M.P. for the Leominster constituency. In 1880, after a rumbustious campaign, Rankin was returned as Conservative M.P. with 457 votes to Thomas Blake's 354, a majority of 103.

After the election, Thomas Blake complained about the behaviour of some of Rankin's supporters saying 'Mr Rankin cannot be ignorant of the extensive treating, bribery, intimidation and undue influence resorted to in order to corrupt the constituency and secure his return'. With Blake's return to his business and philanthropic interests in Ross, Leominster and Parliament lost the services of this good man.

The Redistribution of Seats Act 1885 merged Leominster with the North Division of Herefordshire and at the election of that year, Thomas Duckham was returned as Liberal M.P. for the enlarged North Herefordshire constituency with 3,871 votes to Sir James Rankin's 3,750, a small majority of 121. A year later, Rankin regained his seat when he was elected as Conservative member for North Herefordshire with a majority of 1,693; he went on to retain his seat in the elections of 1892, 1895, and 1900.

LEOMINSTER WORKING MEN'S
CONSERVATIVE ASSOCIATION.
(ESTABLISHED 1876.)

RULES.

I.—The Association shall be called the "Leominster Working Men's Conservative Association." Its object shall be to unite all who hold Constitutional principles in resisting any movement directed against the Constitution of the Country, the Prerogative of the Crown, or the Privileges of the People, as well as to promote beneficial legislation in the spirit of the Constitution.

II.—Any Working man subscribing one shilling per annum, and others as Honorary Members subscribing not less than Five Shillings per annum, to the funds of the Association, may, subject to the approval of the Committee, be admitted a Member.

III.—The Officers of the Association shall consist of the Chairman of the Committee for the time being, and the Treasurer, and a Committee of thirteen Members, who shall be chosen by the Members, at their Annual General Meeting.

IV.—The Committee shall have power to fill up vacancies which may occur in their number, and also to appoint a Secretary, who shall be removable at their discretion.

V.—Five Members shall form a quorum, and the Chairman shall have a second or casting vote whenever the votes on both sides of any question are equal.

Left: *The Leominster Working Men's Conservative Association was formed in 1876 and, to attract the votes of newly enfranchised urban workers, tempted new members with a subscription of only one shilling a year; this Association was to assist Sir James Rankin at the next election in 1880.*

Sir James Rankin, M.P. for Leominster and North Herefordshire 1880–1885, 1886–1906 and 1910–1912

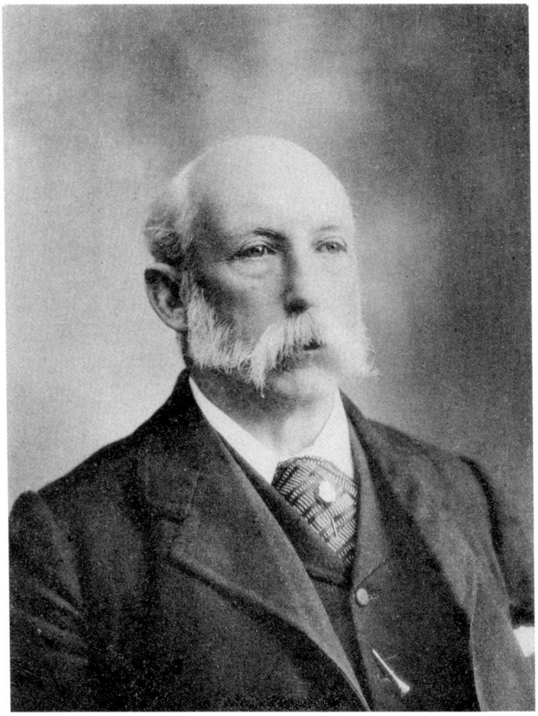

Left: *Sir James Rankin*

Below: *A 1904 meeting in Corn Square when Sir James Rankin used a horse-drawn coach as a rostrum in front of the building that eight years later was to become the Rankin Constitutional Club. Several women in the crowd appear to be leaving, perhaps realizing that his right-wing views opposed any spread of the franchise to women. In the alley in the background workmen clearing the site for the proposed new Post Office ignore the meeting.*

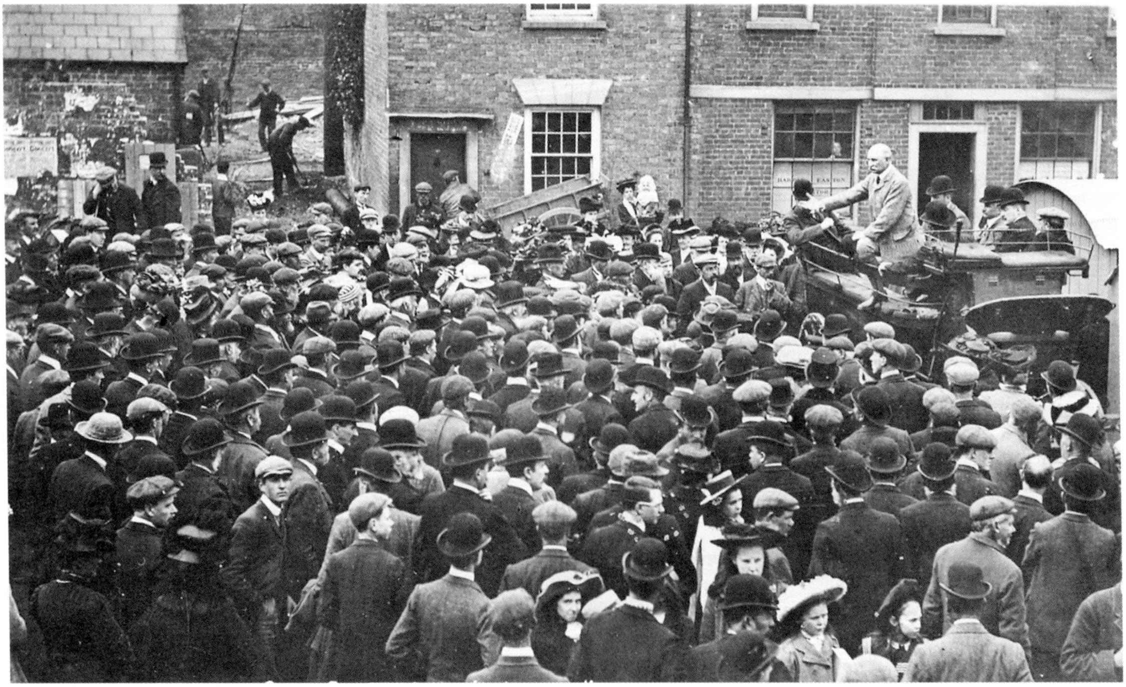

Edmund George Lamb, M.P. for Leominster and North Herefordshire 1906-1910

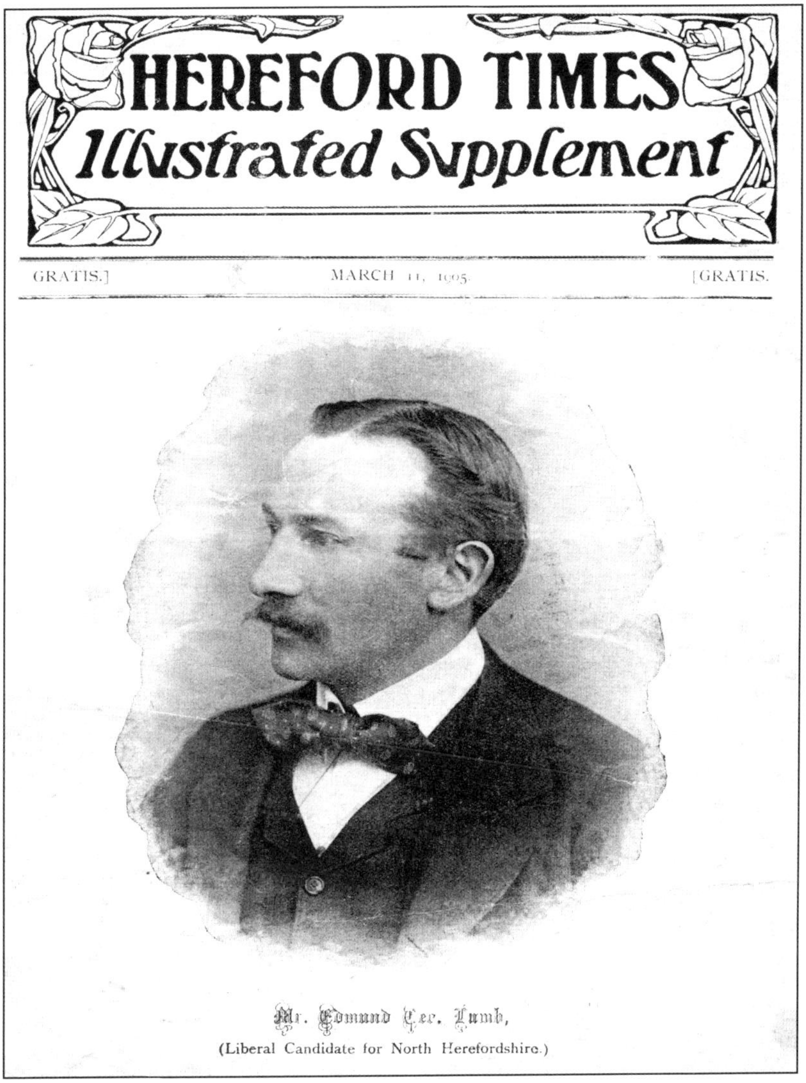

HEREFORD TIMES
Illustrated Supplement

GRATIS.] MARCH 11, 1905. [GRATIS.

Mr. Edmund Geo. Lamb,
(Liberal Candidate for North Herefordshire.)

In the 1906 General Election, Edmund George Lamb, the Liberal candidate, beat Sir James Rankin by a mere 28 votes, on a promise of social reforms; the strengthening of local government; changes to the taxation and rating systems; and reforming the House of Commons. He came from the same type of background as Rankin and also had a degree from Cambridge University. Lamb bred shire and thoroughbred horses on his estate in Borden, Sussex, funded by the profits of his family's Northumberland coal-mining interests. Despite opposition from the House of Lords, the Liberal Government was able to carry out much of its social reform programme in its four years in office. Lamb, however, failed to please the North Herefordshire electorate and in 1910 lost his seat to Rankin by 900 votes.

Municipal Election 1928

Leominster Municipal Election
THURSDAY, NOV. 1st, 1928.
8 a.m. to 8 p.m.

YOU POLL AT
LEOMINSTER POLICE STATION.

Your Register No. is **Nb**....121..........

If you wish to Vote for CHALLIS place a cross against his name as shown below :—

1	**CHALLIS**	**X**
2	GOUGH	
3	KENDRICK	
4	OLIVER	
5	REYNOLDS	

VOTE FOR TOM CHALLIS
The Man you all Know.
He is out to Serve the Ratepayers
He Served King and Country.

Printed by The Leominster Printing Co., and Published by Thomas Challis, 19 & 21, Drapers Lane, Leominster.

There were five candidates for the Leominster Municipal Election in 1928:
Thomas Challis was a butcher at Nos.19 and 21 Draper's Lane;
George Gough was a grocer at No.23 Drapers Lane and No.2 Broad Street;
John Kendrick lived in Hereford Road;
H. Oliver was a fishmonger at No.31 High Street;
and Hubert Reynolds was a grocer at No.14 Broad Street.

This electioneering hand-out issued on behalf of Challis, the butcher, obviously did not have sufficient appeal to the voters as Gough, Kendrick and Reynolds retained their seats on the Council.

The First World War

A

Meeting of Townsmen

WILL BE HELD IN THE

TOWN HALL,

LEOMINSTER,

On Thursday next,

February 24th, 1916,

AT 7-30 P.M.,

To consider Organization in case of

AIR RAID.

The Mayor will preside.

F. A. DALLEY, PRINTER, LEOMINSTER.

In 1915, after 18 months of stalemated warfare, the German High Command directed Zeppelin airships, laden with high explosive and incendiary bombs, to attack British cities to demoralise the civilian population. Each Zeppelin was about 100 yards long and needed a crew of 22 sailors from the German Navy to navigate its deadly cargo to its target. Germany launched 53 Zeppelin and 57 aeroplane raids against Britain and to unprotected civilians they were truly weapons of terror and destruction. Their raids killed 1,413 civilians and injured 3,407 more, mostly in London and the south and east. For defence against these attacks, 20,000 British troops and airmen, armed with anti-aircraft guns and searchlights in support of 12 squadrons of aircraft, had to be deployed in southern England instead of supporting the army fighting in France.

The Mayor of Leominster, Henry Gosling, was persuaded that the risk of attack was great enough to consider plans for emergency action if the town was bombed. In this he was not unduly pessimistic, for Leominster was within range of the Zeppelins' base at Cuxhaven, but in the event it was not attacked during the First World War.

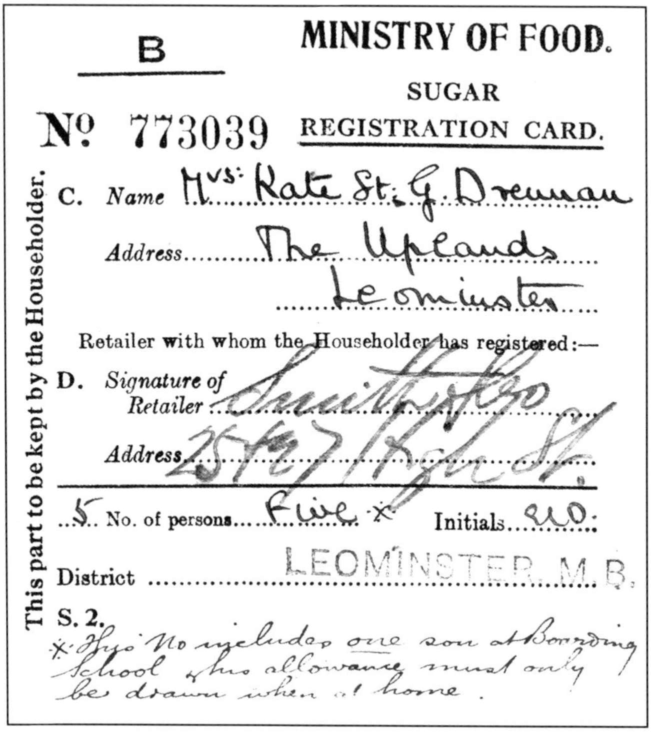

This part to be kept by the Householder.

B

MINISTRY OF FOOD.

SUGAR

No. 773039 REGISTRATION CARD.

C. *Name* Mrs. Kate St. G. Drennan

Address The Uplands

Leominster

Retailer with whom the Householder has registered:—

D. *Signature of Retailer* Smith & Co

Address 25 & 27 High St.

5 No. of persons Five × Initials KO

District LEOMINSTER M.B.

S. 2.

× This No includes one son at Boarding School & his allowance must only be drawn when at home.

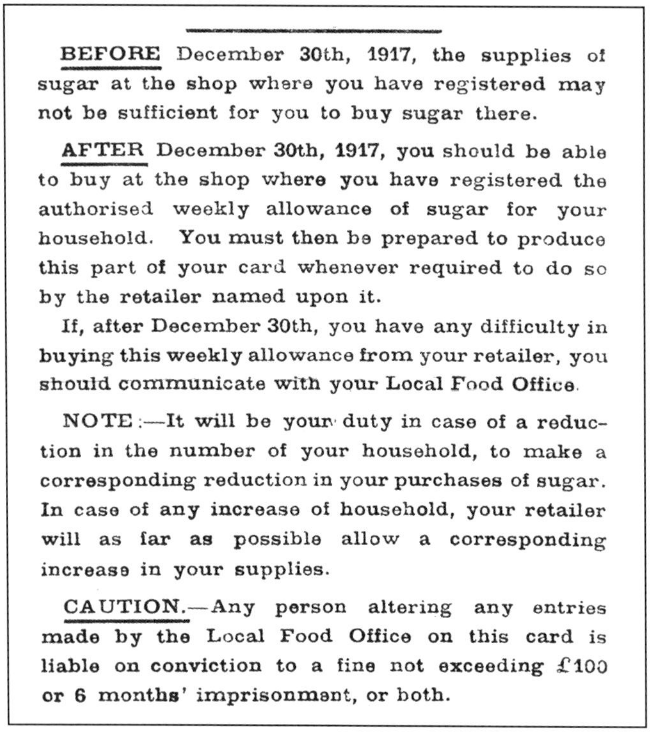

BEFORE December 30th, 1917, the supplies of sugar at the shop where you have registered may not be sufficient for you to buy sugar there.

AFTER December 30th, 1917, you should be able to buy at the shop where you have registered the authorised weekly allowance of sugar for your household. You must then be prepared to produce this part of your card whenever required to do so by the retailer named upon it.

If, after December 30th, you have any difficulty in buying this weekly allowance from your retailer, you should communicate with your Local Food Office.

NOTE:—It will be your duty in case of a reduction in the number of your household, to make a corresponding reduction in your purchases of sugar. In case of any increase of household, your retailer will as far as possible allow a corresponding increase in your supplies.

CAUTION.—Any person altering any entries made by the Local Food Office on this card is liable on conviction to a fine not exceeding £100 or 6 months' imprisonment, or both.

Few ration cards from the First World War survive as a reminder that Britain came within a few weeks of starvation in 1917 due to the number of ships carrying food from America and the Empire that were torpedoed in the Atlantic. A campaign to grow more food, similar to the Dig For Victory drive in the Second World War, was started by the Government with considerable success, with food from gardens and allotments helping to feed the country in the last stages of the war.

This sugar registration card belonged to the Drennan family, who were registered with the long-established grocers, Smith and Co. at 25-27 High Street. Sugar was one of the foodstuffs imported from Australia, the West Indies and the USA and was consequently in short supply. Sugar cane does not grow in our climate, so after the war the Ministry of Agriculture encouraged farmers to grow sugar beet, and manufacturers to build sufficient processing factories to provide a reliable source of home-grown sugar should the need arise. This foresight was appreciated in the Second World War when submarine attacks on convoys were repeated.

LEOMINSTER

RED ✚ CROSS

Carnival & Fete

Thursday, August 8th.

. Programme .

NOTE.—The receipt of many handsome Donations, and Gifts for the Auction Sale to-morrow, will be duly acknowledged in the Press.

DON'T FORGET the
AUCTION SALE To-morrow,
At 2 p.m., in the CORN SQUARE.

PRICE TWOPENCE.

Time Table of Events.

P.M.	
1.30	Carnival Assembly in Etnam Street. *Marshal: C. E. A. MOORE, Esq.*
2.30	Opening Ceremony by Mrs. Clowes, of Burton Court.
2.40	Carnival Judging by the Mayor and Mayoress of Hereford (Mr. and Mrs. Dymond).
2.50	Carnival Awards.
3. 0	**Baby Show** (in Tent). Judges: Mrs. Kevill-Davies and Mrs. Bates.
3.10	The "Monkland Mummers" in Morris Dances.
3.40	Awards and Presentation of Prizes in Baby Show.
4. 0	Gipsy Choir.
4.35	The "Magpies" Pierrots.
4.45	Sports for Munition Girls and Land Girls (arranged by Miss Maddison and Dr. Cressy).
5.20	The "Monkland Mummers" in Country Dances.
6. 0	**Beauty Show.** (Open to all.)
6.45	Archery: Shooting for Winners.
7. 0	The "Magpies" Pierrots.
7.15	Draw for Oil-Painting, presented by the Artist, Miss Mary Moore.
7.20	Draw for Fancy Cake, made and given by Mr. A. Rouch.
7.25	Award and Presentation of Prizes in Beauty Show.
7.30	Draw for Pig, presented by Major Ward-Jackson.
7.45	Draw for valuable Gold Watch.
8. 0	Comic Singing Contest. Judges: Walter Churcher, Esq. and Harry Davis, Esq.,

- Dancing -

Announcements of Awards and Presentation of Prizes will take place from the Band Stand.

The "Magpies" Pierrot Troupe

Of Eardisley.

Miss Doris Jones. Mr. R. J. Roper.
Miss Vera Griffiths. Mr Wilfred Jones.
Miss Olive Jones. Mr. Seymour S. Bourne.
Accompanist: Mrs. J. C. Jones.

Performances at 4.35 p.m. and 7 p.m.

The Monkland Mummers.

Under the Direction of Miss Bengough.

PROGRAMME.

1. Processional Morris
   Leading to
2. Derbyshire Morris Reel.
3. Folk Song (in parts) .. .. "O Waly Waly."
4. Country Dance .. .. "Gathering Peascods."
5. Singing Game.. .. "Looby Light."
6. Country Dance .. "The Old Mole."
7. Flamborough Sword Dance
8. Singing Game .. "A-hunting we will go."
9. Country Dance .. .. "Argeers"
10. Folk Song .. .. .. "The Keeper."
11. Progressive Country Dance .. "My Lady Cullen."

Performances at 3,10 p.m. and 5.20 p.m.

THE GIPSY CHOIR,
Under the Direction of Miss Winterbourn.
Performance at 4 0 p.m.

SPECIAL ATTRACTION!!
Mr. Walter Churcher
The Celebrated London Humorist.

Madame ZENOBIA. The Celebrated Palmist.

SHOOTING GALLERY. | KOKER-NUT SHIES.
HOUP-LA. | AUNT SALLIES.

BAND. Under the Direction of Mr. Fairbanks. | DANCING.

TEAS. * REFRESHMENTS.
Cigars and Cigarettes.

THE DAY AFTER The Fete,

In the CORN SQUARE, Leominster,
AT **2** P.M.

Grand Auction

OF VALUABLE
Household Goods.

There will also be Sold
THE SHETLAND PONY
Generously given by Lord Cawley.

Pigs, Sheep, Lambs, Rabbits and Poultry, from various kind Donors.

The following articles had been given up to last week. Lots more have since been received and still more are expected.

Shetland Pony, or £20 if it does not make this amount; 3 sheep, 1 lamb, several pigs, picture, or £10 if it does not make this amount, set of bowls, 2 mahogany chairs, golf clubs, silver-plated fruit stand, silver-plated teapot, 1 pair of new shoes, lady's saddle, platinum crucible or £10 if it does not make this amount, carpet sweeper, reading lamp, 1 pair of war boots, 1 pair of war shoes, fish servers, leather writing case, rose bowl, biscuit barrel, cupboard, silver-plated coffee pot, coal, brass music stand, woodman's axe, foot stool, work box, work basket, watering can, warming pan, antique silver pepper castor, antique silver patch box, cut glass scent bottle, 1 dozen each Port, Sherry and Champagne glasses, pair of decanters, biscuit box sauce tureen, celery glass, copying machine, deck chair, flower table, gipsy table, mounted horns 2 fenders, 2 watches, carved hall stand, firewood, pipe rack, poultry, easy chair, honey, 2 table cloths, pewter jugs, sewing machine, Worcester china plate, salt cellars in case, rush dress-basket, silver cream jug, brass candlesticks, gramophone and records, china jug, 10 vases, tame rabbits 9 pictures, flower stand, trays and table ornaments, scent bottles, book and d'oyley, tea, butter, cockerels, silver spoons, eggs, silver photo frame, zither, antique vases, harness, saddle, dish covers, silver brooches and bangle, butter dish, looking glass, parcel of clothes, cruets, melodion, silver bracelets, 4 pipes and 2 tobacco pouches, 2½ dozen toilet soap, silver-plated butter knives, spoons, etc., parcel of socks, ties, etc., jam, potatoes, cushion covers, 6 pre war loaves, 9 coat hangers, collar for donkey, curtain poles, cake knife, water bottle.

Come and Buy!!

¶ The Committee press for your favourable consideration the cause of the NATIONAL EGG COLLECTION FOR WOUNDED SOLDIERS.
Whenever you are asked by the Collectors to give—either of Eggs or Money—***Give Freely***

Money raising events proliferated in every town and village as the effects of the war were felt. To fund its work with wounded soldiers, Leominster Red Cross organised a Carnival and Fête on 9 August 1915, to be followed the day after by a massive Auction Sale in Corn Square. The programme cost 2d.

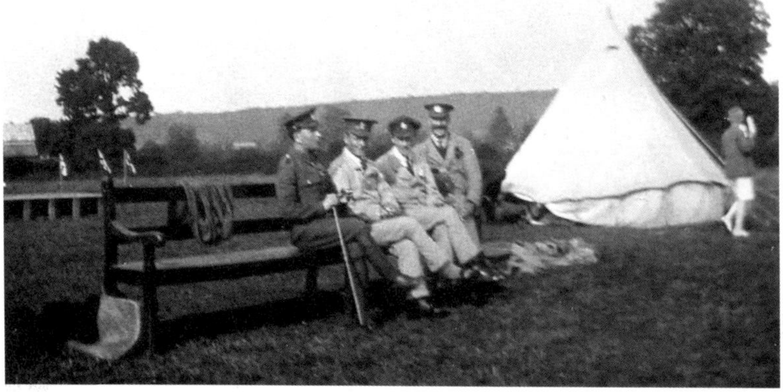

Left: *Convalescent soldiers in their hospital uniforms are seen here enjoying a pleasant afternoon at the Grammar School sports day in 1916 or 1917. Visits to ordinary social events like this were encouraged to help them forget some of their experiences in the trenches. These men were patients at Mrs. Burrough's mansion at Hampton Court, which in 1915 she had turned into a convalescent hospital for wounded soldiers.*

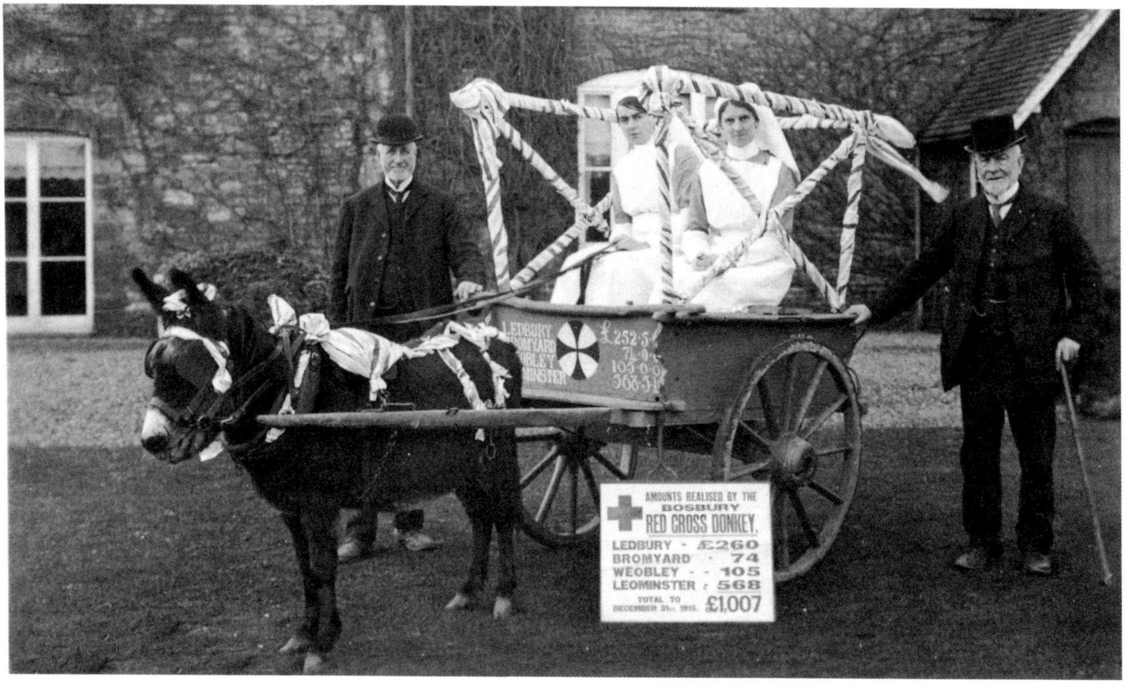

Above: *In 1915 Bosbury's Red Cross donkey cart was taken to fund-raising events around the county, collecting over £1,000. Suitably decorated with flags and bunting, it took part in Leominster's Carnival, where the Lane sisters, both Red Cross nurses from Bosbury, helped collect a very creditable £568 for their fund. The Red Cross ran several of the convalescent hospitals in local country houses in addition to its relief work in war affected areas.*
The old donkey died in 1916 after raising over £3,000.
The cart is said to be safely stored in a dry barn.

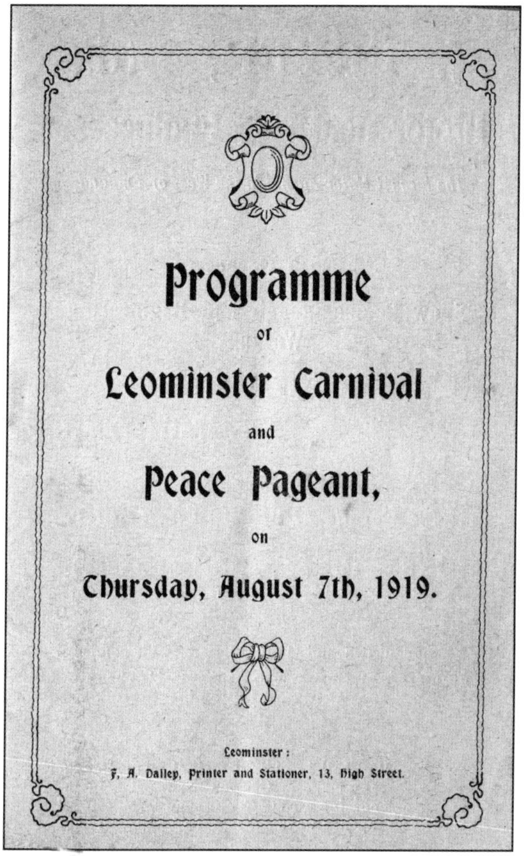

Programme
of
Leominster Carnival
and
Peace Pageant,
on
Thursday, August 7th, 1919.

Leominster:
F. A. Dalley, Printer and Stationer, 13, High Street.

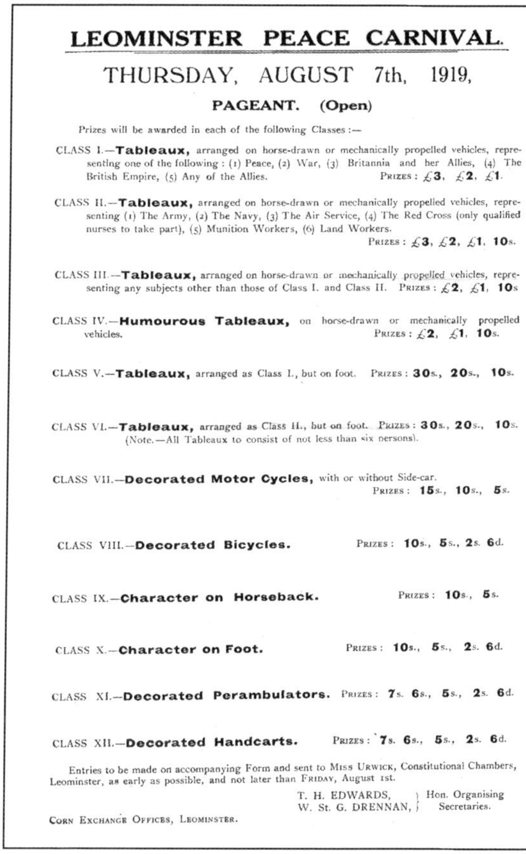

LEOMINSTER PEACE CARNIVAL.

THURSDAY, AUGUST 7th, 1919,

PAGEANT. (Open)

Prizes will be awarded in each of the following Classes :—

CLASS I.—**Tableaux,** arranged on horse-drawn or mechanically propelled vehicles, representing one of the following : (1) Peace, (2) War, (3) Britannia and her Allies, (4) The British Empire, (5) Any of the Allies. PRIZES : £3, £2, £1.

CLASS II.—**Tableaux,** arranged on horse-drawn or mechanically propelled vehicles, representing (1) The Army, (2) The Navy, (3) The Air Service, (4) The Red Cross (only qualified nurses to take part), (5) Munition Workers, (6) Land Workers. PRIZES : £3, £2, £1, 10s.

CLASS III.—**Tableaux,** arranged on horse-drawn or mechanically propelled vehicles, representing any subjects other than those of Class I. and Class II. PRIZES : £2, £1, 10s

CLASS IV.—**Humourous Tableaux,** on horse-drawn or mechanically propelled vehicles. PRIZES : £2, £1, 10s.

CLASS V.—**Tableaux,** arranged as Class I., but on foot. PRIZES : 30s., 20s., 10s.

CLASS VI.—**Tableaux,** arranged as Class II., but on foot. PRIZES : 30s., 20s., 10s.
(Note.—All Tableaux to consist of not less than six persons).

CLASS VII.—**Decorated Motor Cycles,** with or without Side-car. PRIZES : 15s., 10s., 5s.

CLASS VIII.—**Decorated Bicycles.** PRIZES : 10s., 5s., 2s. 6d.

CLASS IX.—**Character on Horseback.** PRIZES : 10s., 5s.

CLASS X.—**Character on Foot.** PRIZES : 10s., 5s., 2s. 6d.

CLASS XI.—**Decorated Perambulators.** PRIZES : 7s. 6s., 5s., 2s. 6d.

CLASS XII.—**Decorated Handcarts.** PRIZES : 7s. 6s., 5s., 2s. 6d.

Entries to be made on accompanying Form and sent to MISS URWICK, Constitutional Chambers, Leominster, as early as possible, and not later than FRIDAY, August 1st.

T. H. EDWARDS, W. St. G. DRENNAN, Hon. Organising Secretaries.

CORN EXCHANGE OFFICES, LEOMINSTER.

Above left: *J.B. Dowding was Mayor for an unprecedented four years from 1917 to 1920. One of his most pleasant jobs was to plan the programme for Leominster's Peace Carnival on 7 August 1919. This was undertaken with the help of a committee superintended by W.St.G. Drennan and T.H. Edwards. They even persuaded Gaumont (a cinema news company) to make a film of the day's events, and it was screened a week later in the Picture Palace.*

Dowding was a respected councillor, public auditor and J.P., yet only five years after organising this popular event, believed to be the biggest Carnival Leominster had ever seen, he was declared bankrupt, then convicted of embezzlement and fraud, and sent to prison for four years.

Above right: *An entry form for the Peace Carnival, The Grand Draw attracted the main interest as the first prize was a new £250 five-seater Ford motor car for the cost of a 2s. 6d. draw ticket. The winner was a 12-year-old boy from Dilwyn. The other 77 prizes ranged from a fountain pen to sheep, pigs, chickens, a camera and a Shelley bowl.*

Over £1,000 was raised towards the cost of Leominster's war memorial.

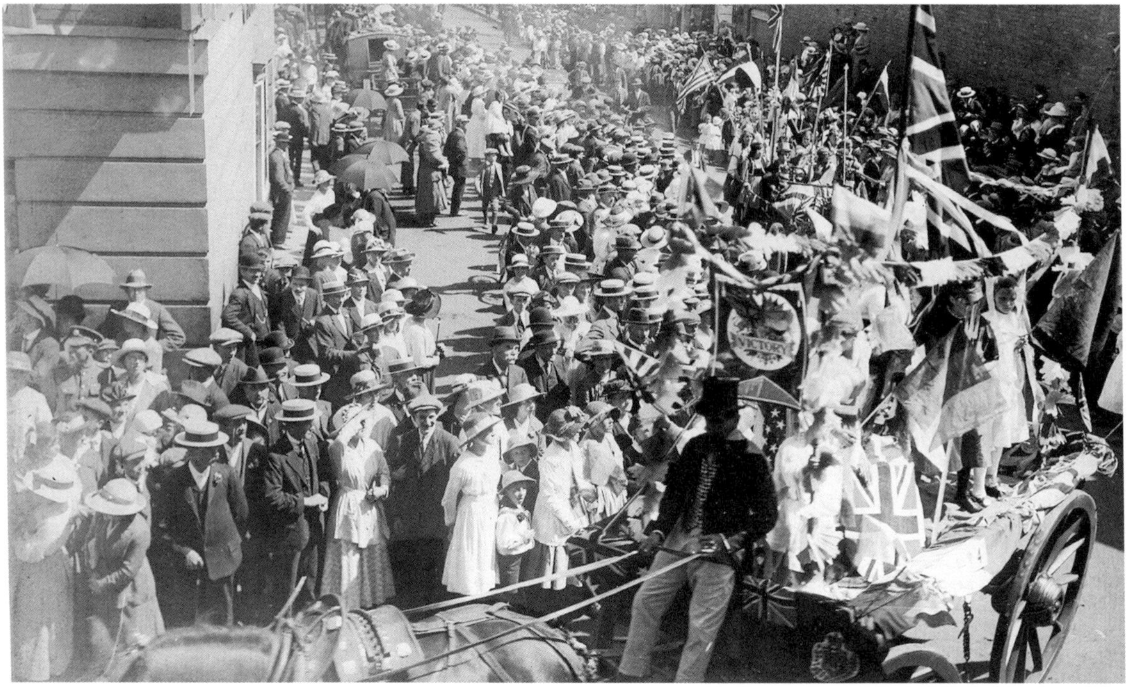

Above: *At 1.30 pm in hot summer sunshine the Peace Procession filled Etnam Street as it commenced its slow parade round the town on its way to Eaton Hill Park, where Mrs Burlton, the owner, officially opened the celebrations. Here over 10,000 people from the county and beyond rejoiced that the awful war years were finally over and were entertained with music, side shows and athletic races.*

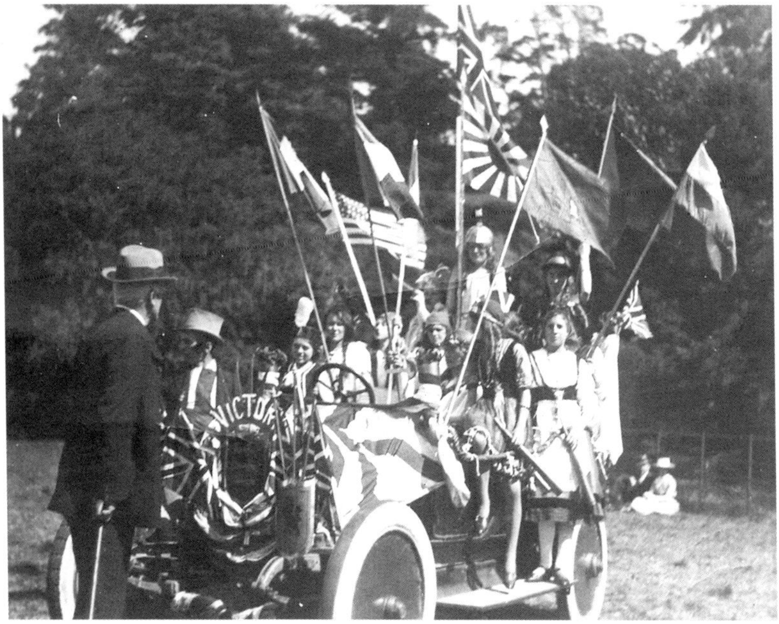

Left: *Taking part in the peace procession was the entry from the Grammar School 'Britannia with her Allies'. This colourful flag-bedecked car won second prize of £2 for its youthful occupants.*

Royal Events

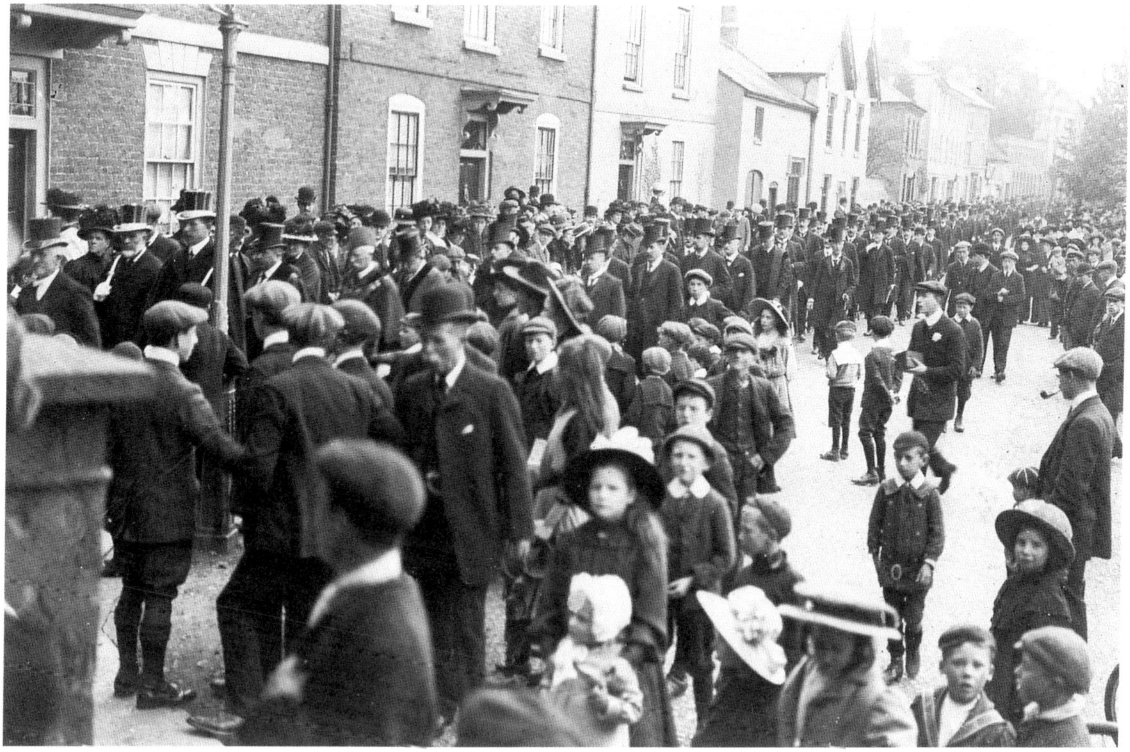

The townspeople gathered to watch the suitably robed and top-hatted civic dignitaries process from the Town Hall, along Church Street, to the Priory Church for a service of commemoration for King Edward VII, who died on 10 May 1910. Despite his zest for living and his questionable private life, Edward was a popular king. In general, people regarded him as a peacemaker between his argumentative European relations.

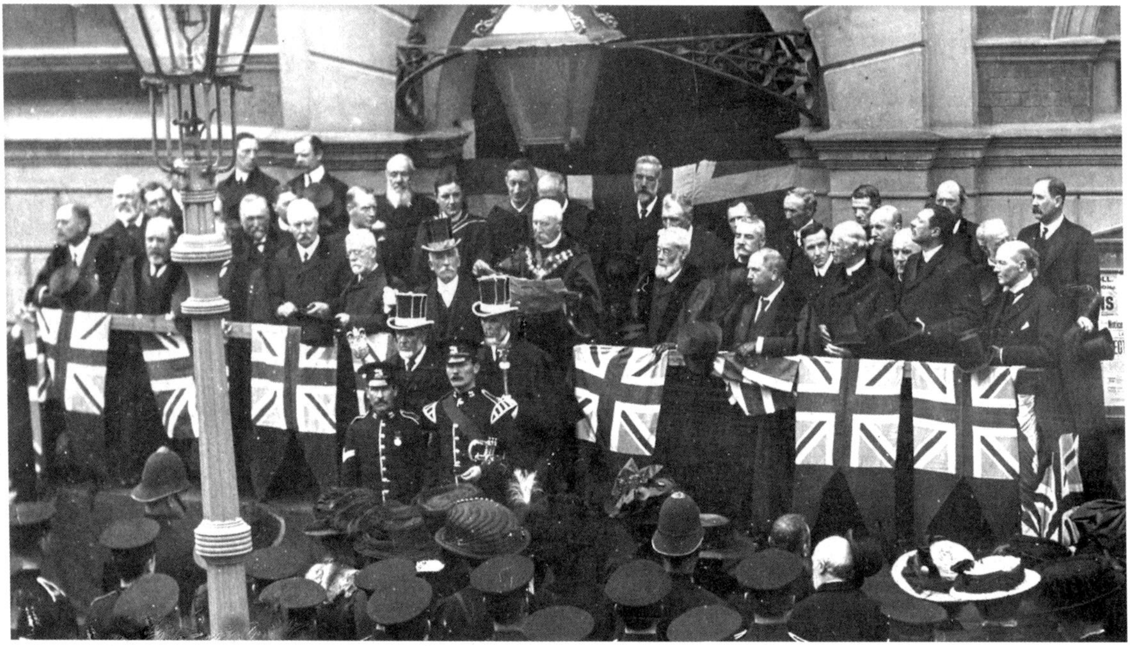

On May 11 1910, from a temporary flag-covered dais erected in front of the Town Hall, J.G. Abell, Leominster's Mayor, proclaimed King George V's accession, watched by the town's dignitaries and an honour guard of local men from 'F' Company of the 1st Herefordshire Regiment.

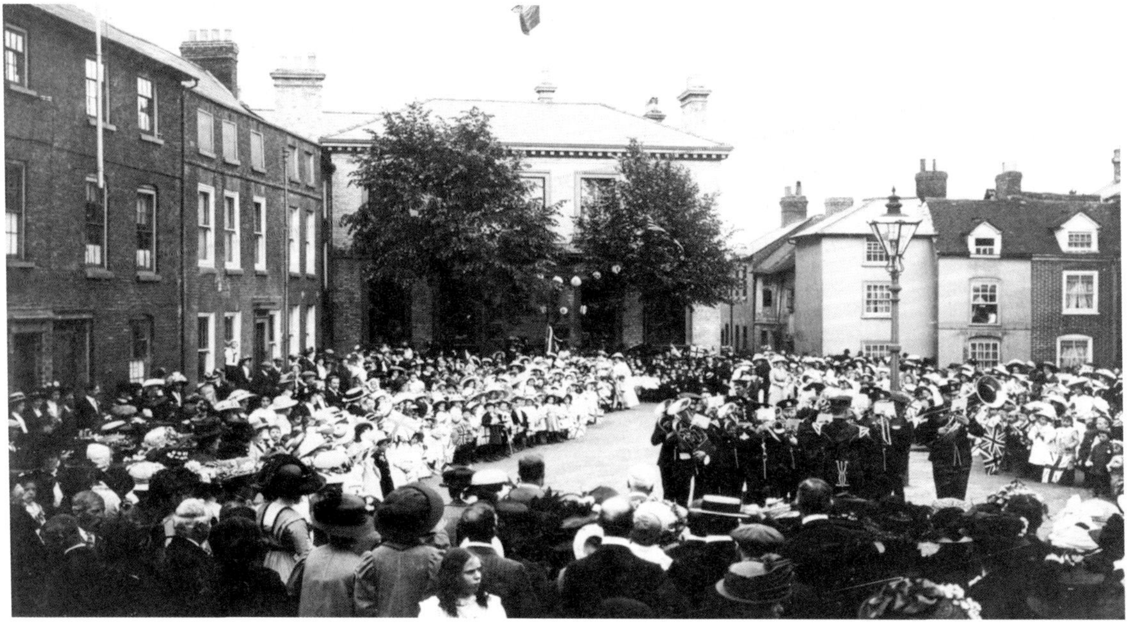

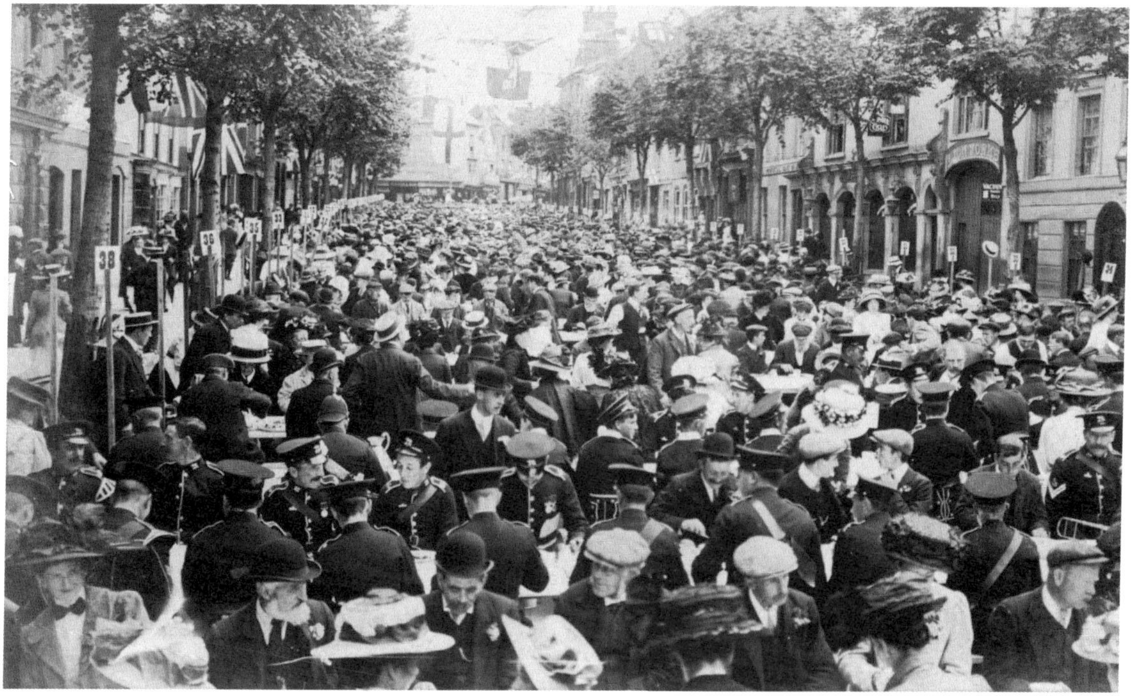

Above: *Some of the 1960 people who bought tickets for a celebratory meal to mark King George V's Coronation in far-away London. A six foot high temporary wooden fence isolated Broad Street and a police constable was stationed at each of the four entrances to allow only ticket holders entry. Sharp on time the diners sat down to their meal and consumed 1,206 lbs of roast beef, 1,960 penny loaves and 1,000 lbs of plum pudding, washed down by an unrecorded quantity of free beer and cider. For the teetotallers the Women's Temperance Association provided tea or lemonade. Meals were sent to the old and infirm who could not attend in person.*
Although published by De'Ath this photograph was taken by W.C. Miles, standing on a tall step ladder to get the necessary height and angle.

Left: *It appears that Lloyds Bank was the only building in Corn Square that had hung up a few flags to add some colour for the crowds enjoying the Coronation festivities to the music of the town band. At three o'clock the crowded square watched as nine hundred children assembled to march with the band to Broad Street for their tea and buns at four o'clock.*

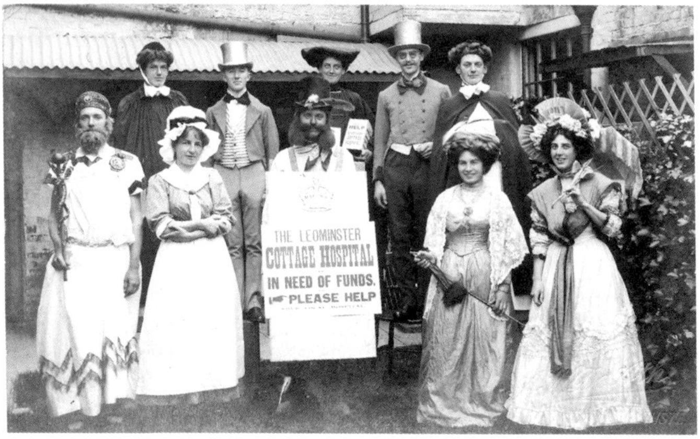

Left: *Before the establishment of the National Health Service in 1948, fund raising for Cottage Hospitals was a perennial problem and Leominster's £1,500 hospital, built in 1899, was no exception. Taking advantage of the Coronation celebrations, some supporters of the local hospital dressed up and collected what they could from the crowds.*

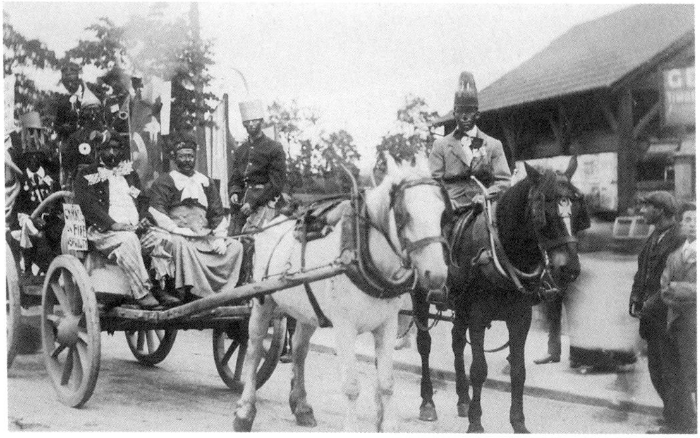

Left and below: *Some of the floats in the Carnival parade assembled in George and Tudor's timber yard at No.90 Etnam Street, whose buildings are visible in the background. The local fire brigade blacked their faces and donned strange costumes to become the 'Darktown Fire Brigade'.*

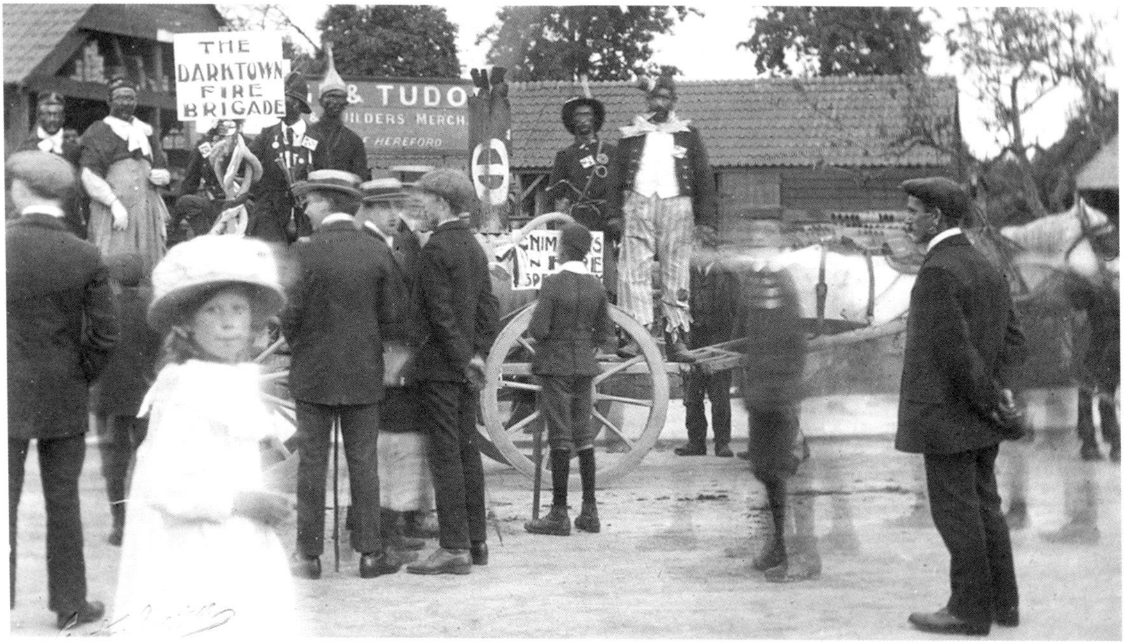

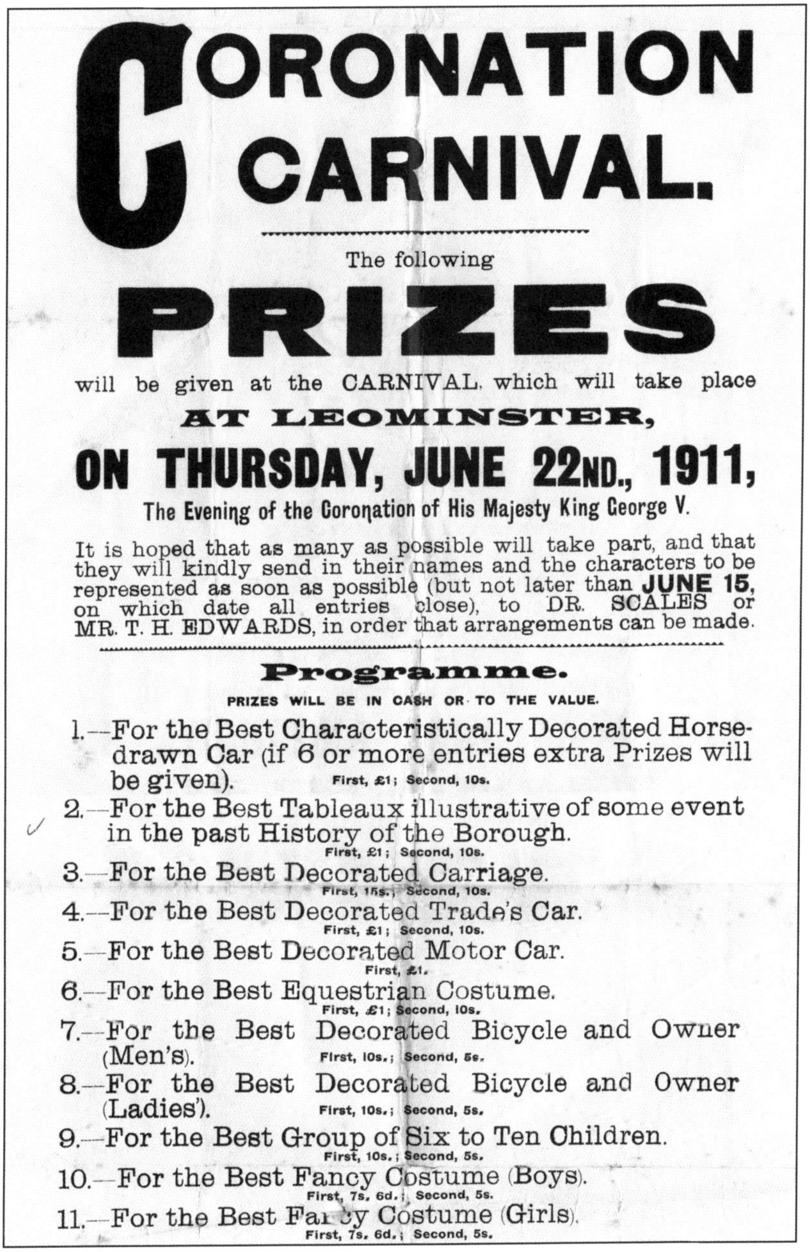

CORONATION CARNIVAL.

The following

PRIZES

will be given at the CARNIVAL. which will take place

AT LEOMINSTER,

ON THURSDAY, JUNE 22ND., 1911,

The Evening of the Coronation of His Majesty King George V.

It is hoped that as many as possible will take part, and that they will kindly send in their names and the characters to be represented as soon as possible (but not later than **JUNE 15,** on which date all entries close), to DR. SCALES or MR. T. H. EDWARDS, in order that arrangements can be made.

Programme.

PRIZES WILL BE IN CASH OR TO THE VALUE.

1.—For the Best Characteristically Decorated Horse-drawn Car (if 6 or more entries extra Prizes will be given). First, £1; Second, 10s.

2.—For the Best Tableaux illustrative of some event in the past History of the Borough. First, £1; Second, 10s.

3.—For the Best Decorated Carriage. First, 15s.; Second, 10s.

4.—For the Best Decorated Trade's Car. First, £1; Second, 10s.

5.—For the Best Decorated Motor Car. First, £1.

6.—For the Best Equestrian Costume. First, £1; Second, 10s.

7.—For the Best Decorated Bicycle and Owner (Men's). First, 10s.; Second, 5s.

8.—For the Best Decorated Bicycle and Owner (Ladies'). First, 10s.; Second, 5s.

9.—For the Best Group of Six to Ten Children. First, 10s.; Second, 5s.

10.—For the Best Fancy Costume (Boys). First, 7s. 6d.; Second, 5s.

11.—For the Best Fancy Costume (Girls). First, 7s. 6d.; Second, 5s.

A 1911 Coronation Carnival poster. Leominster's Mayor, J. Biddle, sanctioned the Town Council's donation of £200 to the Entertainment Committee to fund the celebrations for King George V's Coronation. A programme of events commenced with an Anglican service in the Priory Church, which was followed by a united open air service on the Grange. The festivities continued with a dinner for 2,000 people in Broad Street at 1.15 pm; sports at the Grange at 3 pm; and a children's tea in Broad Street at 4 p.m. The proceedings were rounded off with an evening carnival, bonfire and fireworks.

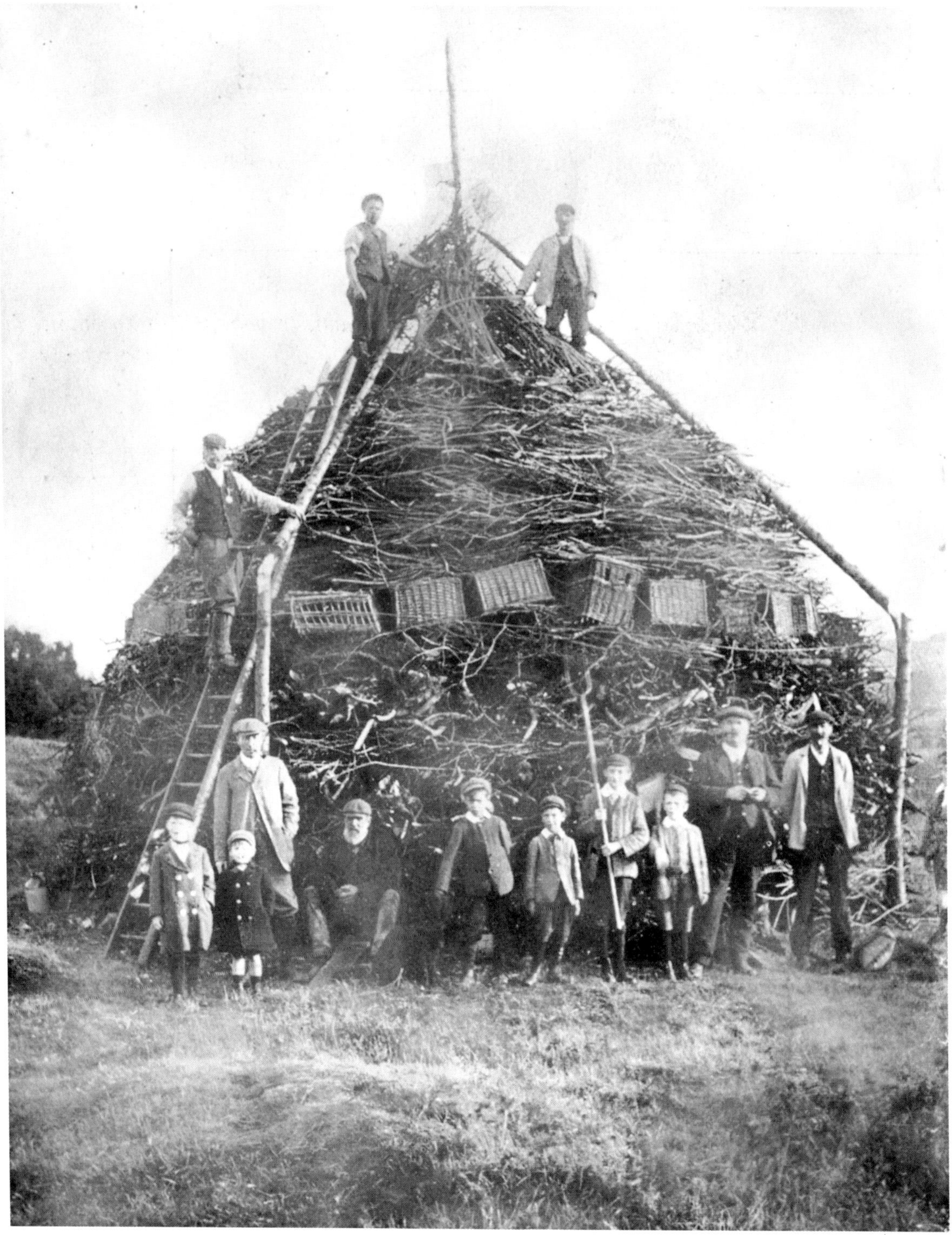

Building the 1911 coronation bonfire on Pound Field.

Sport

LEOMINSTER

MUNICIPAL STAKES.

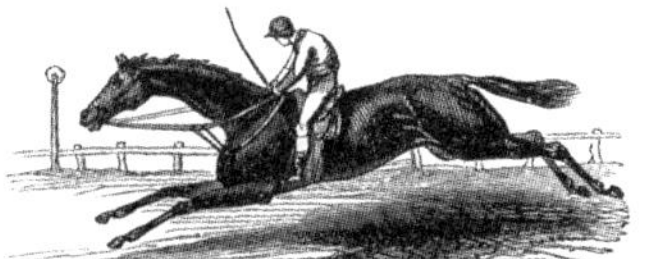

TO BE RUN OVER THE OLD BURGESS COURSE, ON THE 1st NOVEMBER, 1913.

Sport is meant to be fun and this delightful spoof race card from 1913 was used for an event designed to raise money for the local hospital.

The humour is to be found in the names of the runners (below left) *and some, probably personal, references known only to the local community.*

LIST OF STARTERS AND JOCKEYS.

OWNER. CANDIDATE. JOCKEY.

1.—Mr. Beerbohm Tree's "**Liver Complaint,**" by "Dexterity," out of "Clear the Way" .... Mr. Forceps.

2.—Mr. Gilbey's "**Jack of all Trades,**" by "Axe to Grind," out of "Ulterior Motive" .... Mr. Turbot.

3.—Mr. Kipper's "**Sly 'un,**" by "Bankruptcy," out of "Distraint" .... Mr. Fagg.

4.—Mr. Knowall's "**Ignoramus,**" by "Strikeleader," out of "Socialism" .... Mr. Smelter.

5.—Mr. Nevercome's "**Tea Caddy,**" by "Lime Juice," out of "Quaker Girl" .... Mr. Lamp-Placer.

6.—Mr. Gift o' the Gab's "**Varsity Charlie,**" by "Large Panel," out of "Good Practice" .... Mr. Farmer's Union.

7.—Mr. Weighbridge's "**Scrap Iron,**" by "Old Clothes," out of "Ragtime" .... Mr. Cobbler.

PLACE BETTING (THURSDAY EVENING).

3 to 1 on Varsity Charlie.
2 to 1 on Jack of all Trades.
Evens Tea Caddy.
2 to 1 against Liver Complaint.
3 to 1 against Scrap Iron.
50 to 1 against Sly 'Un.
100 to 1 against Ignoramus.

As the betting shows VARSITY CHARLIE and JACK OF ALL TRADES are strong favourites for 2 of the 3 places. The former is quite a popular fancy for the leading position. His breeding counts for a lot and as the old adage has it, "class will tell." He has not done any severe training for the race but his friends assert (and they should know) that he does best on a light preparation. He can safely be trusted to get the course and his owner and jockey are two of the best. JACK OF ALL TRADES is best described as a "dark horse." Horses of this description are as a rule best left alone by backers until their public performances have proved them worthy of support. He has, however, been well trained on the splendid gallop adjoining the Cemetery and as the stable have put their money down on this occasion, it would be folly not to follow the lead thus given. SLY 'UN seems hopeless. He has never yet been placed in a race, but on one occasion enjoyed the good fortune of a walk over. It helped to pay the Corn Bill. He should be turned out of training and thus save the public further disappointment and expense. LIVER COMPLAINT is another candidate of good class but is not of too tractable a nature. Being a bit headstrong he is likely to "get off" badly and with such a big weight to carry that may prove fatal. Given a good start he is likely to run into a place. TEA CADDY has been well backed by his connections. Although his training has been of so short a duration he will make the best of them gallop when it comes to racing, and may be safely trusted to get the course. It should be a good race between him and Liver Complaint SCRAP IRON has a "coming appearance" in the market but his owner and jockey are both inexperienced in racing of this class. He has not been trained in the orthodox manner for such a trying contest, but his friends nevertheless seem hopeful. IGNORAMUS would do better at a flapping meeting and his claims on such an occasion as this are not worth consideration. Like all others of his class he will finish with the "also ran."

LATEST CLUB BETTING (FRIDAY NIGHT).

5 to 1 on Varsity Charlie and Jack of all Trades.
Evens on Tea Caddy and Liver Complaint.
8 to 1 against Scrap Iron.
66 to 1 against Sly 'Un.
250 to 1 against Ignoramus.

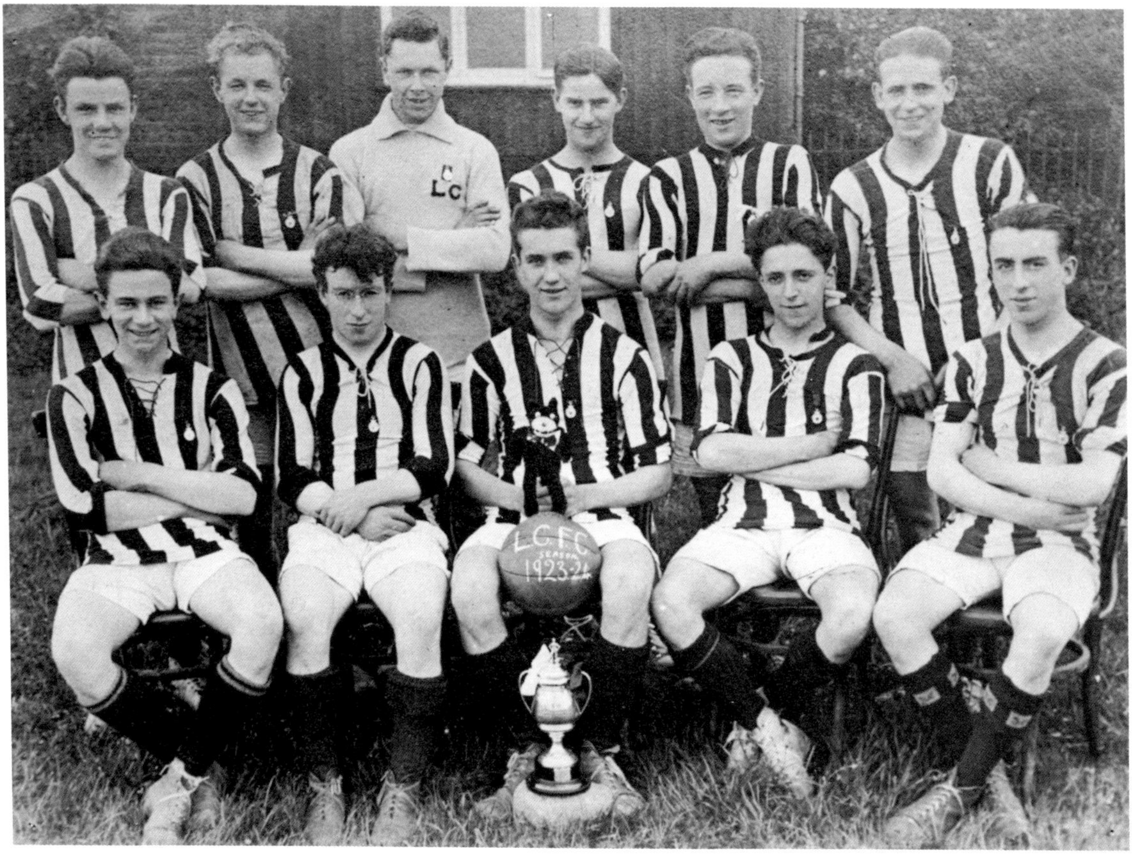

Above: *Leominster CFC 1923–24 Team Photo*
Back Row: T. Evans, D. Seager, F. Skingley, O. Owen, F. Rutter, A. Stephens.
Front Row: I. Bannister, E. Reynolds, W. Hodges, W. Preece, C. Reynolds
all wearing the medals they earned for winning the Cup.

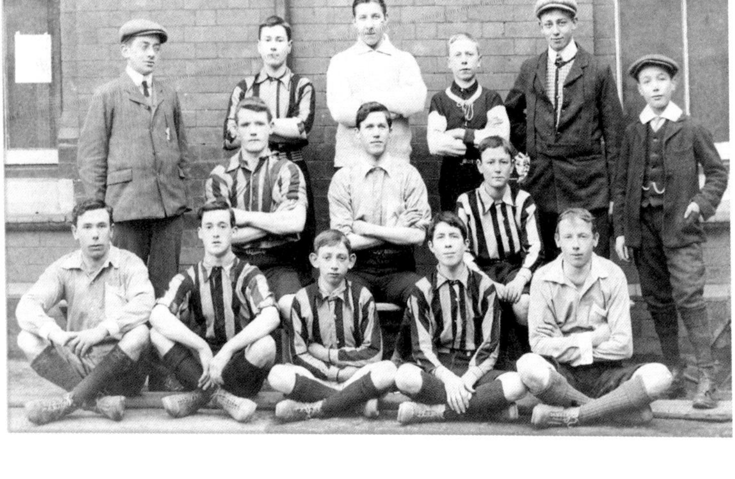

Left: *Leominster G[range] FC 2nd XI 1907–8.*

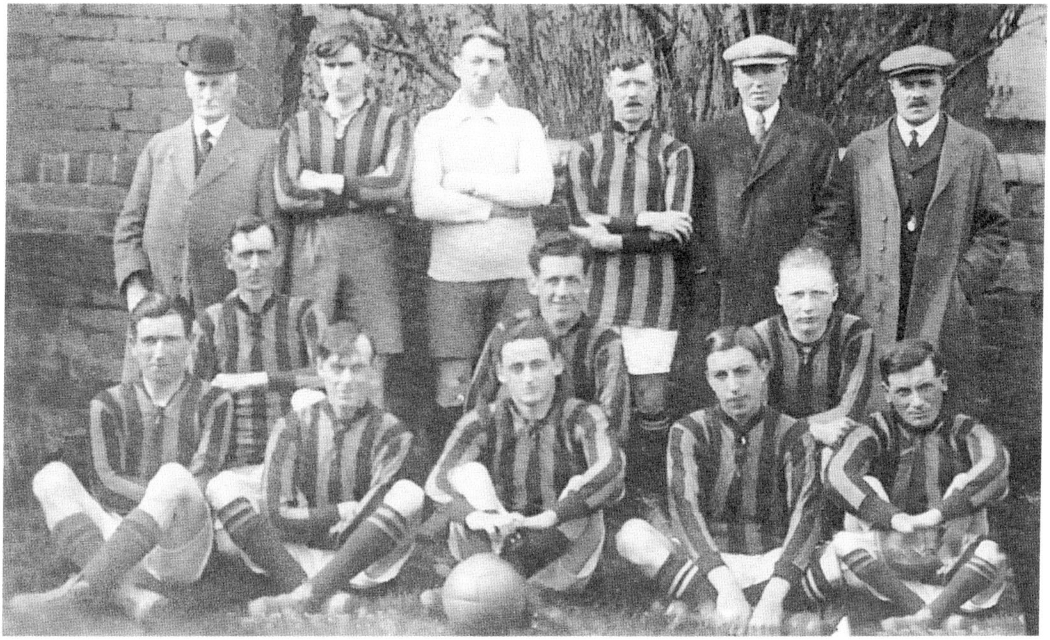

The Leominster Post Office football team in 1925.
On the reverse is a note 'Postmen 4 Railwaymen 1'.

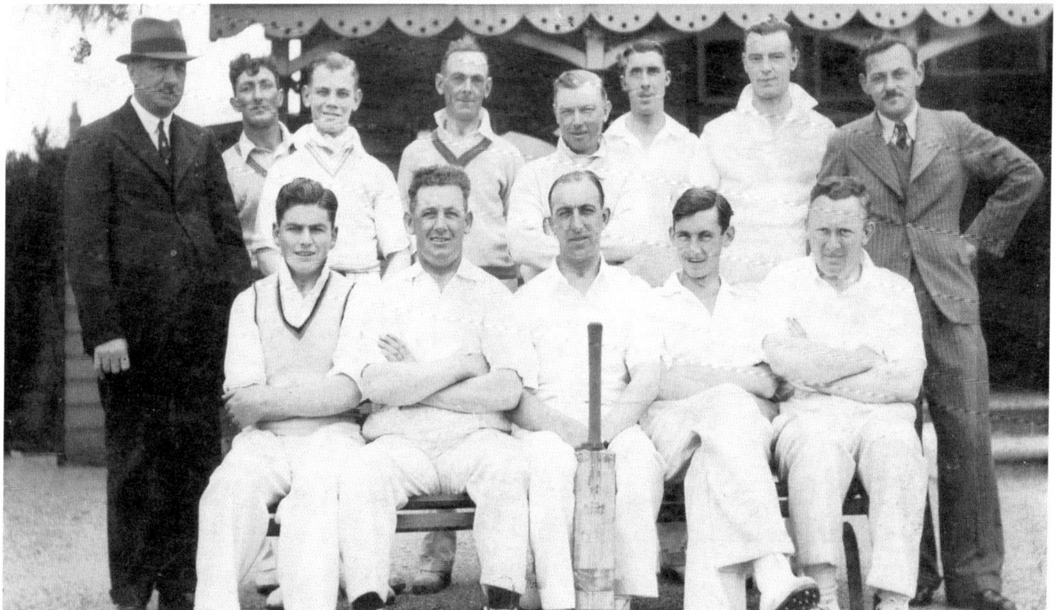

Leominster Cricket Club in the 1920s, photographed outside their pavilion at the Grange, which was built in 1901.
Back row: ? , ? , Powell Jun., Powell Sen., ? , Thomas, ? , ? .
Front row: ? , Nicholas, Preece, ? , Hams, ? .

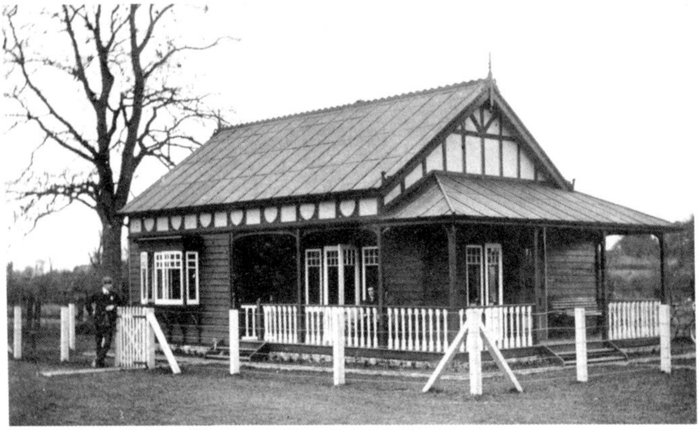

Left: *Leominster Golf Club, which was incorporated in 1903, first played on a course near Kingsland sawmills, where a nearby house is still called the Golf House, acting as a reminder of the club's presence. Sometime about 1905, the club moved to a course near Steens Bridge Railway Station, where they bought and erected this pavilion on hire purchase. In 1909,* Kelly's Directory *lists E.P. Lloyd of No.28 South Street as the club's secretary. However, the* Leominster News *reported in April 1921 that the Revd G. Walter and H. Reynolds were joint secretaries, H. Gosling captain and H.R. Harding treasurer. Harding said that he had to announce that there was still a £38 mortgage on the pavilion and a £22 deficit from the previous year. Even so, members voted by a narrow margin to continue playing. No one knows the reason but after about thirty years the club moved again to their present attractive course at Ford Bridge and took their pavilion with them. It was re-erected on a slight rise in front of the present club house. By the 1960s when the club was revived it had become nearly derelict.*

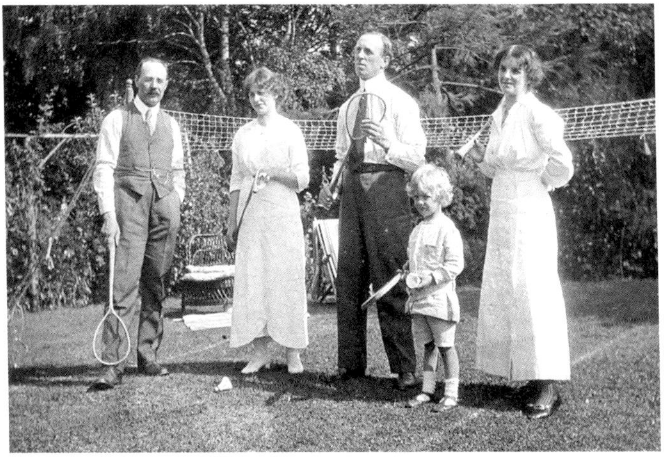

Left: *Today badminton is normally considered to be an indoor sport. However, it also has also a history as an outdoor activity, as this informal Edwardian photograph of the Drennan family playing at their home at Uplands shows. They evidently played here regularly, as the properly marked out lines and the net suspended behind their shoulders seem to be a permanent court. Their approach to the game, however, was quite casual. It must have been a pretty gentle pastime; one of the gentlemen is still wearing his watch chain, waistcoat, collar and tie. Sleeves are not rolled up and ordinary shoes are the order of the day. The old wooden racquets look like museum pieces, and they would have weighed considerably more than modern alloy ones, putting a lot more strain on the wrist.*